To: Angie & Bob
Thanks for your

"Enjoy your journey"

Jim Mitchell

Journey Of A Baby Boomer 3-30-2000

Doug, Buddy, and Me
Tailgating at Jordan-Hare

Journey
Of A
Baby Boomer

Jim Mitchell

Keego House Publishing
Auburn, Alabama

Published by
Keego House Publishing
P. O. Box 1375
Auburn, AL 36831

Journey Of A Baby Boomer
Copyright © 1999 by James F. Mitchell, Jr.

James F. Mitchell, Jr.
2510 Wildwood Drive
Auburn, AL 36832

All the material contained in this publication is either original or has been collected from public domain sources. Credit has been given to the individual believed to have originated the material.

First Edition, 1999

ISBN: 1-928784-08-9

Cover design by Mike DeMent

Printed in the United States by:
Morris Publishing • 3212 East Highway 30 • Kearney, NE 68847
1-800-650-7888

To my brothers, Buddy and Doug,
who helped make my journey
exciting:

To my parents, who cared more and
shared more than I ever realized;

To my sons, Jimmy, Doug, and Ben
my special blessings from God;

To Anne, who has always believed in
me .

Acknowledgments

This book took over three years from conception to actual completion. Many people have helped in the process. Family and friends have provided encouragement, expertise, suggestions and support in various ways. Thanks, everyone for being there when I needed you.

I am grateful for the feedback and editorial help from my friend Amy Stephenson Hall. Amy spent numerous hours helping me prepare the final manuscript. Thank you, Amy.

Mike DeMent, a good friend and fine artist, designed the cover for the book. His creative vision, talent, and dedication to his work is endless. Thanks, Mike.

I want to thank all my clients and the audiences who have inspired and encouraged me over the years. Thank you, all.

Table of Contents

Introduction

In January 1996, I celebrated my fiftieth birthday. I had not looked forward to the event. To me it meant the end of life as I have known it. But despite my protests, it happened.

Over the years both minor and major changes had occurred in my physical body, and I was not prepared for any more traumatic *stuff* to develop. For instance, my muscles fit much looser now than they once did, my eye sight is not as good, my hair is thinner, my hearing is going and it takes me much longer to get moving each day.

I now have **senior moments**. Those are the times when I have trouble remembering what transpired yesterday or even an hour earlier. But I have learned to conquer the problem of forgetting. I keep appointment books, notes and calendars. This should help me remember, but then I forget where I placed the things I use to help me remember.

I can remember many events that occurred in past years, but the present is often not as clear.

Perhaps that is the way it was meant to be. Regardless, events of years gone by are indelibly printed in my memory. I enjoy reminiscing about the "good ole days," but try to erase the bad or uncomfortable days.

Turning fifty does have its advantages. I can now take **Centrum Silver** legally, get my own **AARP** card (I don't have to use my wife's anymore), and get a free checking account at my local bank.

As a *baby boomer*, I won't be alone for very long. According to statistics, between the years of 1946 and 1964, 76 million individuals were born known as *"baby boomers"*. Beginning January 1, 1996, at least two individuals classified as *baby boomers* will turn 50 years old every 7.5 seconds.

Boomers helped make fashion statements, influenced the election of our politicians, changed the English language, and established norms for the types of music to which America listens.

As a member of the baby boom generation I have witnessed the assassination of a United States' President, the British invasion of 1964, the Vietnam War, man walking on the moon, the birth of the computer age, and I witnessed the powerful influence of television and threat of nuclear power on my world.

I grew up in an era of unparalleled prosperity. I witnessed the movement of people and businesses

10

from cities to suburbs, which prompted a building boom in housing, schools, and shopping malls. Many in my generation were part of the youth rebellion and counterculture movements of late 1960's, some were committed to the civil rights movement and others opposed the Vietnam War.

I am part of the most affluent generation the world has seen. I will live longer than previous generations and have more opportunities for success than anyone ever imagined. As a baby boomer I experienced the Civil Rights movement, Watergate, runaway inflation, double digit interest rates, economic boom, and the highest standard of living the world has ever seen; yet many in our generation are hungry and homeless.

Now as I begin the second half century of my life I tend to reminisce more than ever about what life used to be like. As the Lone Ranger said at the beginning of each new episode, *"Return with me now to the thrilling days of yesteryear"*.

The Second Half Of Life

I knew I had turned fifty years old:

●When coffee became one of the most important things in my life.

●When I entertain, my neighbors don't realize I am having a party.

●When I started making donations to Public Television.

●When I began watching a lot of *adult television* (the Weather Channel, the Home and Garden Channel, the Food Channel and the History Channel).

●When my friends or children call at 9:30 PM and ask "Did I wake you?"

●When I can grow hair on my ears, but not on my head.

●When I quit trying to hold in my stomach when an attractive lady walks by.

●When people who look older than me began to call me "Sir".

●When I remember when made in China and Japan

meant it was junk or wouldn't work.

● When my children started to make more money than me.

● When I no longer went the Barber shop, but to the hair stylist praying for a miracle.

● When I saw old friends at my high school reunion and they said "you haven't changed a bit".

● When my new car cost more than my first house.

● When I began spending several hours a day watching birds feed in my backyard.

● When I discovered a closet full of ties but wouldn't throw them away because they may come back in style.

● When I started taking medication that I only thought old people took and I couldn't even pronounce the names of the *prescriptions*.

● When I started throwing away things and later found out they were collector's items.

● When my friends started telling me, "you are not getting older, you are only getting better".

● When my medicine cabinet wouldn't hold any more prescriptions (some of them expired ten years ago).

● When my mail started to consist of burial insurance, extended health care, and diet enhancement advertisements.

●When I received a "senior citizen" discount and didn't have to show proof of age.

●When started to wake up before dawn, no matter what time I went to bed.

●When I had trouble falling asleep at night, but could sleep through any minister's sermon.

●When I could remember when tennis shoes cost $6.95 (The same shoe is now called a jogging shoe and sells for $79.95).

●When my children wanted to hear me talk about the "good ole days".

●When my boys started listening to me and asking my advice.

The Age of Innocence

The Way Things Were

The years from 1946 to 1958 might be classified as our *years of innocence*. These were the years when I was pretty much sheltered from the events of the real world. Television coverage of world events was not as graphic and not every home actually had a television set, therefore I got much of my information from the radio. At that time in my life, I was more interested in radio episodes of the *Lone Ranger, Green Hornet, Amos and Andy, Gunsmoke, Arthur Godfrey* and *Queen For A Day* than late breaking news coverage.

I can remember the day when I was fishing in

15

"my tub" on the back porch when the radio broadcast reported news of events taking place in Korea. I asked Bertha (our housekeeper from 1946 to 1951) "what was Korea?" She said, "Korea is a place over the ocean where everybody is killing everybody." To this day, I can't think of a better definition of war.

Mom and Dad would read bedtime stories and nursery rhymes to Buddy, Doug, and me. We would listen and could actually visualize the places and characters mentioned on the pages. One of my favorites was "Jack and the Beanstalk". I still have the picture in my mind of the giant chasing Jack down the beanstalk and Jack cutting the beanstalk down before the giant could reach him. In those days, we used our imaginations to make pictures from the words in the stories.

During our years of innocence we made our own fun. Television was not an option for us since there were only a few stations broadcasting in our area and televison sets had not taken their place of authority in the home. We fashioned weapons from tree branches, built make-shift forts and hideouts, and played army or cowboys and Indians riding horses made from old brooms or mops. We allowed our imaginations to run wild and we had good clean fun.

Diseases such as measles and mumps always seemed to strike around the holiday season. If one of us got sick, Mother always put us together in a dark room so the light would not cause us to become blind and so the measles and mumps would not spread to the rest of the family. She figured we would all come down with them sooner or later, so it might as well be sooner.

During the summer months, Mom always made us take a nap during the heat of the day. It was her way of protecting us from polio which was a major threat to children as we were growing up. After lunch, she would lay down with us to help us rest. At least that is what she told us. On days when we couldn't rest, we would get up, slip out of the bedroom and leave Mom sound asleep. Today we call them power naps. Mom was just ahead of her time.

My major mode of transportation was the bicycle. I traveled everywhere on it. To make my bike sound like a real motorcycle, I attached a playing card or piece of cardboard to the spokes with a clothes pin. This made the spinning bicycle wheels create a motor like sound that could be heard a block away.

I leaned to read from books centered around the adventures of *Dick, Jane and Spot*. Your place in reading groups indicated how well you could read. Each week I got to read to the teacher which gave me the opportunity to move up to a more accelerated group if my reading proficiency improved.

Teachers used various colors to identify the

reading groups. Blue was for the best readers, red was for the average reader, green was for weak readers, and brown was for the poor reader. I think I was in the red reading group most of my grade school years.

Young Entrepreneurs

My brothers and I sold Kool-Aid and lemonade from small store front stands we built. Our advertising effort took the form of hand written signs such as:

```
For Sale
Kool-aid & Lemonade
2¢ a glass
```

As youngsters raised during the 1950's, becoming successful businessmen and making big money were our goals. We tried everything from kool aid stands and newspaper routes, to selling "Grit" newspapers and Christmas cards. Our parents had to bail us out more times than we could count. We just never hit on the right business as youngsters. Then in 1958 I finally saw potential for big dollars without much overhead.

19

The product was mistletoe. It grew in many of the trees near our house in Ft. Smith, Arkansas and all I had to do was get it down, wrap it in ribbon and sell it to people to use for Christmas decorations. To help with the business venture, I recruited my brothers, Buddy and Doug.

The plan was simple, we would knock the mistletoe out of the trees, wrap it with ribbon, and sell it door to door for five cents a bunch.

Sales were not very brisk, in fact after twelve or thirteen houses we were in the process of quitting. Then Buddy and I had a brilliant marketing idea. We decided that Doug, the youngest, would do the selling.

Doug was "hard of hearing" and wore hearing aids that resembled our present day portable radio. With wires running from the power supply to his ears he would always win the heart of even the hardest *Scrooge*. After several objections by our youngest brother, we convinced him it was the best method to apply in our desperate situation.

We changed our approach. We sent Doug to each door with the mistletoe and Buddy and I would hide nearby. For the several hours, we watched and encouraged Doug, and the sales were great. In fact, we ran out of the product and had sales of over $5.00 for our effort.

We had to replenish the supply of our product

20

so we returned home to prepare for the biggest sales push ever in the mistletoe market. But, as you might suspect Mother found out what we were doing and put an end to the *"Big Business Venture"*.

We have worked together on other ventures through the years, but nothing was as sweet and successful as the "Mistletoe".

Eventually new products were added to our business enterprise to include old comic books and unwanted baseball cards.

Comic Books and Baseball Cards

Comic books could be bought for 5¢ at the local *"Dime Store"* and every grocery store sold Baseball cards for 5¢ a pack. Collecting both comic books and baseball cards was important to us. Each pack of baseball cards contained 5 to 10 pictures of current players and a flat piece of bubble gum. I can remember getting both Stan Musial and Mickey Mantle cards one summer.

Baseball cards were traded between family and friends. Cards of greats such as Al Kline, Willie Mays, Richie Ashburn, Stan Musial, Ernie Banks, Don Larson, Whitey Ford, Roy Campanella, Yogi Berra, Sandy Kofax, Ernie Banks, Hank Aaron, Eddie Mathews, Mickey Mantle, Don Drysdale, and Duke Snyder were usually the most difficult to get. Even as a young boy I knew that some were more valuable than others, but little did I realize what some of those cards would be worth forty years later.

Television

There wasn't much television when I was growing up. Most of the programs aired in the afternoons and evenings. All the television sets were black and white and there was no such thing as a remote control. Any kid on the block who had a television set in their home became very popular.

The first program I remember watching was Abbott and Costello in 1952. We were living in Alaska at the time and a friend had a television set. The screen was tiny and the reception was not the best compared to today's standards, but we didn't know the difference. Buddy and I watched the program in amazement--we couldn't believe they had a *picture show* in their house. Little did I know then the impact television would have on my life and my generation.

In July of 1954 we moved from Alaska to Louisville, Kentucky, and dad bought a television. In 1956, all of America watched Davy Crockett on television. He was the "king of the wild frontier" and my hero. I sang the "Ballad of Davy Crockett" and watched every episode that came on television. Coon skin hats were in great demand and anyone fortunate enough to have one was the envy of the neighborhood.

23

I can remember watching programs after school such as Howdy Doody, Superman, Lassie, and the ever popular Mickey Mouse Club. The Mousketeers were the stars and of course Annette was my favorite Mousketeer. All the boys wanted her as their girl friend and all the girls wanted to be her. The episodes of *Spin and Marty* which were shown on the program were an added treat.

The words to the Mickey Mouse theme song still ring clear after forty years.

"Who's the leader of the club

That's made for you and me?

M-I-C-K-E-Y M-O-U-S-E!

Hey, there! Hi, there! Ho, there!

You're as welcome as can be!

M-I-C-K-E-Y M-O-U-S-E!

Mickey Mouse! Donald Duck!

Mickey Mouse! Donald Duck!

Forever let us hold our banners high!

High! High! High!!

Come along and sing a song

And join the jamboree

M-I-C-K-E-Y M-O-U-S-E!

(Then very slow)

M-I-C See ya real soon!

K-E-Y Why? Because we like you!

M-O-U-S-E!

Remember, you had to be there to appreciate what Walt Disney's program meant to our *years of innocence*.

Saturday Morning Television

Saturday morning was television day for me. The programs were entertaining, educational and included cartoon festivals, westerns and variety shows. I sat and watched *Tom and Jerry, Tom Terrific, Mighty Mouse, Bugs Bunny, Daffy Duck, Porky Pig* and *Popeye The Sailor.* I watched *Captain Kangaroo, Howdy Doody, Hopalong Cassidy, Gene Autry, the Cisco Kid, Roy Rogers, Kit Carson, Wild Bill Hickok, Annie Oakley, Superman,* and *the Lone Ranger.*

I remember how John Reid, a Texas Ranger, was shot in an ambush, left for dead and was nursed back to health by Tonto. He was the only Ranger to survive and changed his name to the Lone Ranger. To hide his identity he decided to wear a mask and fight for justice using silver bullets. Silver was the name of his horse and Scout was Tonto's horse. Together they made a terrific team.

The Roy Rogers show with Dale Evans, Trigger and Buttermilk, along with Bullet (the dog) drew everyone to the television on Saturday. Roy and Dale lived at the "Double R Bar Ranch" near Mineral City. They had a jeep named Nellybelle. Together they got the bad men and you could usually count on

Roy to sing a song on most episodes.

Eventually Sky King (the flying cowboy) and his niece Penny became one of my favorites. There was always Sergeant Preston of the Yukon and his dog King. Lassie eventually moved to Saturday morning to join the Rin-Tin-Tin series. Of course, all these programs were in black and white.

My first exposure to direct mail came in the mid-1950's. Captain Midnight was one of my Saturday morning heroes. He wore a special decoder ring. The ring enabled him to decode secret messages and made him a powerful force in the battle for good in the evil world. The decoder ring was offered to viewers who would send in a certain number of *Ovaltine* seals. Advertisements from other programs encouraged you to buy certain cereals and save the box tops for prizes. Sometimes prizes would be found in specially marked boxes of cereal while *Cracker Jacks* always offered a special prize inside each box.

I remember the *Lone Ranger* doing commercials for Cheerios and other General Mills products. *Sergeant Preston* promoted Quaker Puffed Wheat and Puffed Rice which were shot from guns, *Roy Rogers* endorsed Post Sugar Smacks, and *Superman* did commercials for Kellogg's cereals. Guy Madison who played *Wild Bill Hickok* pushed Kellogg's Sugar Corn Pops while Gene Autry chewed Wrigley's chewing gum.

Parents were not immune to the influence television advertising was beginning to have on America. Grown ups saved *S&H Green Stamps, Gold Bond* or *Top Value* stamps in little books which they could redeem for merchandise. Many families would only shop at grocery stores or buy gas where their favorite stamps were given. I can remember licking a lot of stamps to put into those little books. It was a family thing.

Television in the evenings and at night was very limited, but provided families with good wholesome entertainment. We watched Father Knows Best, Ozzie and Harriet, Leave It To Beaver, and Make Room For Daddy. I am still amazed, after raising three boys of my own at how those homes we saw on television could always look so neat and clean. Somehow these programs helped reinforce the principles of right and wrong, fairness, integrity and good manners which I was taught at home by my parents. Emphasis was placed on the home and what we refer to today as *"family values"*.

In addition to these, the comedy programs of *Burns and Allen, The Honeymooners, The Real McCoys, I Love Lucy, Jack Benny, Red Skelton, Milton Berle,* and *Sid Caesar* kept us laughing. Later, quiz shows such as *Twenty One, I've Got A Secret, What's My Line,* and *The $64,000 Question* became night time viewing favorites. Programing during the day included the popular *Queen For A Day, The Price Is Right*, and of course *Soap Operas*.

Among my favorite programs were *I Remember Mama, My Little Margie, Our Miss Brooks*, and *Topper*. In the mid fifties, westerns like *Cheyenne, Gunsmoke, Wyatt Earp, Bat Masterson, The Rebel, Rawhide, The Rifleman, Maverick, Wagon Train, Bonanza, Zorro*, and *Have Gun Will Travel* received my viewing attention. On Friday night, the entire family watched boxing matches with Dad on "The Gillette Cavalcade of Sports".

"Mamie"

Her name was Sally. But to all of her grandchildren she was Mamie. Mamie and my grandfather (Pappy) Mitchell lived and raised their family in Scotts Hill, Tennessee. Pappy died in 1953 when we lived in Alaska.

Since we lived in many places during the 1950's and 60's we were only able to visit Dad's family when he received a transfer or took leave. The town had a theater, jail, school, and several small family owned stores. By today's standards there was not much opportunity for excitement. But my Uncle Henry and my cousins always entertained us in the most innovative ways.

We fished, played Cowboys and Indians, listened to Saint Louis Cardinals baseball games on the radio, and heard stories about the Mitchell family. My brothers and I always looked forward to going to the livestock sale. Since we had grown up on Army Posts and in cities, this was a big thrill. We were not accustomed to seeing cows, pigs and horses everyday. We called this event going to the zoo. When our visits took place during the winter Uncle Henry took us to hog killings and barbecues.

Mamie always got up before daylight to cook breakfast. Since my brothers and I slept in the same big bedroom with her, we would often get up to watch her. It was on one of those cold early mornings that she first introduced Buddy, Doug and me to coffee. Even though we were young fellas she saw no harm in allowing us to drink it. She would pour about ¼ cup of coffee in our cups and fill the remainder of each cup with milk and add plenty of sugar. Since Mother didn't approve of young boys drinking coffee, Mamie would have to sneak it to us. Of course she didn't fool Mother, but then, Mothers always know everything that is going on.

Buddy's Rooster

Breakfast at Mamie's was really a feast. She made biscuits every morning, cooked ham, bacon, sausage, eggs, grits, and usually had fried chicken along with great hot coffee. One of the most exciting things the visiting *city grandsons* did with her was to go to the hen house and help gather eggs.

Mamie cooked the best fried chicken in the state of Tennessee. She raised her own chickens, no store-bought birds for her. One day we watched her go to the chicken yard and get a chicken for dinner. She wrung its neck, plucked the feathers, cleaned it and then cooked the chicken. We had never seen anything like that and were amazed that she could do all that by herself.

Buddy wanted to help Mamie with her chores. He had witnessed the scene when she selected a chicken and then prepared the bird for dinner. He decided to help with dinner the next day. He went to the chicken yard and ran down a chicken just as Mamie had done the previous day. He tried to wring its neck and when he found that too difficult, he chopped it off with an axe.

Uncle Henry was the first to see Buddy coming

32

from the back yard. He couldn't believe what he saw. There was Buddy proudly holding the chicken he had killed for dinner. Now, in our brief chicken yard instruction, nobody told us the difference between chickens and roosters. In his excitement, Buddy had selected Mamie's prized rooster for the dinner meal.

I don't remember how that fried rooster tasted. But I will always remember the day Buddy tried to help our grandmother. As I look back at my visits to Scotts Hill, I now realize that everything she did and every meal Mamie prepared for us, was done out of her love for Mom, Dad, Buddy, Doug and me.

"Maw Maw"

We called her "Maw Maw" but to everyone else in Brewton, Alabama she was Mrs. Hill. Even though she married Ray Estabrook late in life, many in this South Alabama town still referred to her as Mrs. Hill.

Maw Maw opened *The Ritz Cafe* in Brewton in 1940. The Ritz was located on heavily traveled Highway 31. Since this was the main artery from the North to the South, people from all over the United States would stop at the Ritz to dine.

In 1952 she opened a new restaurant called Marlane's approximately one-half mile south of the Ritz Cafe on the other side of Burnt Corn creek. We were living in Alaska at the time and we only knew about the new venture from pictures Maw Maw sent. Her move proved to be successful. Business was good as several civic clubs held meetings, the locals became loyal customers and travelers would stop to enjoy a good meal in her modern restaurant.

Maw Maw offered curb service. Each booth in the restaurant had a coin operated music selection machine that linked into the juke box. You could select your favorite song for 5¢ or 6 songs for 25¢.

34

Maw Maw knew how to advertise. She knew if you provided a great meal in a well maintained establishment people would spread the word. Her philosophy was "do what you do so good, that people can't resist telling others about you." Her main method of attracting traveling customers came in a very innovative way.

She utilized a long time employee by the name of Emmett. He became the restaurant's most famous celebrity. Emmett would stand in front of Marlane's wearing a white coat and hat ringing a dinner bell. As he rang the bell at lunch time he would point at the restaurant. He attracted many traveling down Highway 31 South and became one of Brewton's main attractions in the 1950's. Of course Maw Maw's fried chicken and biscuits really drew the crowds.

The Eagle Drive-In

In the 1950's and 1960's there were over 4,500 drive-in theaters across the United States. They were open air theaters where you could watch movies from your car. The Eagle Drive-In was located in East Brewton, Alabama. You paid 50¢ to $1.00 per car to watch a movie. It was an ideal place for family outings. My parents took me and my brothers in our pajamas. Mom and dad didn't have to dress up or find a baby sitter to enjoy an evening out.

I can remember when the family station wagon was the best seat at the movies. Dad would clean the windshield and we would load up the car with our favorite snack food. Dad would pull the car up on the little berm next to other cars, hook up the speaker to the outside window and we would wait for the movie to begin. Then we could all enjoy the feature in the privacy of our own vehicle.

When it got dark enough, things started to roll. The big outdoor screen provided previews of coming attractions, Movietone news, short subjects, and a cartoon. I was more interested in the cartoon than the actual feature. Sometimes we were allowed to go to the playground located near the refreshment center.

The boomer generation was very innovative and quickly utilized initiative to find that drive-in theaters were not only for family outings. It was a great place to socialize with friends or take a date. Since the theaters were outside, rain often threatened to ruin the evening and no one wanted to watch a movie with the wind shield wipers on. To teenagers, rain posed no problem because often we weren't really there to watch the movie.

Today less than 500 drive-in theaters grace our land and the *Eagle Drive In* no longer exists, but the memories will last forever. Our children don't know what they missed.

Brewton Elementary School

My Dad was in the Army and we moved frequently. I attended several elementary schools during my years of innocence and each one has a special memory or two. When my Dad was assigned to Korea, my mother and father moved the family back to our home town of Brewton, Alabama. We lived with my grandmother for the two years that my dad was in Korea. I attended Brewton Elementary School for the fifth and sixth grade.

Each morning when the roll was called we were allowed to purchase a carton of milk to drink during our morning break. We could bring a snack from home to eat as we drank our milk. This was an opportunity for us to kick back and allow our brain cells to absorb all the knowledge shared with us by Mrs. Ida Liles. It was a nice break.

It was an honor to be chosen to go to the cafeteria and get the morning milk for your class. I really don't remember why, but I do know all of us looked forward to being selected for the daily milk run. This was part of our daily routine and came prior to recess.

We always looked forward to recess. It gave us an opportunity to go outside and play football, baseball, or kick ball with our friends. Unfortunately, when it rained, we were stuck indoors. In an effort to control our energy on those wet days, Mrs. Liles would plan activities and often teach us songs. The songs were really fun to sing and we didn't mind doing singing since we couldn't go out anyway.

We sang *"Row, Row, Row Your Boat"*, *"The Erie Canal"* and several other songs. The words of my favorite songs are still engraved on my mind after forty years. They were known as *"Found A Peanut"* and *"The Deacon Went Down To The Cellar To Pray"*.

Terror In The Sky

On October 4, 1957, the Soviets launched the world's first satellite, Sputnik. Americans were frightened by the news. The Russians had beaten us into outer space. It was determined by those in power that school children must concentrate on math and science if we were to move ahead of them in technology in the years ahead.

Until that day, the only thing we knew about space flight was gleaned from Buck Rogers on the movie screen. Now, my generation was caught up in the "race for space". Fall out shelters were the rage as Americans made plans for a possible Russian invasion or nuclear attack. Khrushchev's statement, "History is on our side. We will bury you!" didn't make us feel very secure in the "land of the free and the home of the brave".

We lived under the threat of a Russian invasion. Several public, underground locations were designated as civil defense shelters and they were marked with yellow and black signs. We were taught to go there in the event Russia dropped the bomb.

Adding to the Russian scare was the launch of Sputnik II in November that carried a dog on board.

40

Age Of Innocence

It wasn't until Alan Shepard went around the Earth in May 1961 that I really started feeling better about our situation. In the mean time, I was bombarded with more and more math and science to do my part to help America get and stay ahead of the Russians in the *"race for space"*.

The Ritz Theater

The Ritz Theater had a Saturday morning and afternoon matinee every weekend. The price of admission for kids under 12 years old was 15¢, but everyone else had to pay 50¢. I couldn't wait to turn 13 so I could pay 50¢ and not be seen as a kid any longer. Little did I know how much that additional 35¢ meant to my parents in those days.

We called the theater the *picture show*. We waited in line and saved places for our friends so we could all go in together to see our heroes of the silver screen come to life. Once we got inside we were usually there for the entire afternoon. I remember nervously watching the clock on the wall as the hands moved slowly to the time for the show to begin. When the curtains finally opened to reveal the screen, there was a loud cheer from everyone.

Above the seats in the balcony, light from the projection room displayed the movie on the screen. Cartoons came first, then *Movietone News*, followed by previews of coming attractions, then the serial, and finally the feature. Some Saturdays there would be a double feature and that meant we would be in the picture show all afternoon. When we walked outside it took several minutes for our eyes to adjust to the light.

Among my favorite heroes of the Saturday serials were Captain America, Captain Midnight, Superman, and Buck Rogers. The action packed moving pictures were shown one chapter at a time in weekly installments. We would speculate all week about what would happen next. It was all we could do to wait for next Saturday to roll around.

It just didn't get any better than sitting in the picture show with my brothers and our friends sharing a box of popcorn, eating a giant size candy bar and drinking a Coke. The experiences that I had on Saturday mornings in the *Ritz Theater* are treasured memories. I can still hear the six guns firing, see the burning arrows flying through air and Lash La Rue using his famous whip to bring down the bad guys. There are so many times I wish I could do it all over again.

Billy's Guitar

In 1957 I was only 11 years old, but "Rock & Roll" was beginning to make an impression on me. I listened to my favorite tunes that had been recorded on 45 rpm records or to my favorite radio station. The local radio station in Brewton was *WEBJ* and was the only station I could pick up at that time. Each evening the station had a call-in show. My friends and I would call the station and request a song and dedicate it to a girlfriend or a group of friends. The music we listened to began to prepare us for our *teenage* years.

His name was Billy Townsend. Billy lived on Douglas Avenue across from the High School football field (Rotary Field). The girls in my 6th grade class thought he was the best looking boy around. He had long brown hair and dark blue eyes, and he had a guitar. Mr. and Mrs. Townsend owned the *Town House Restaurant* in downtown Brewton. Billy had a record player and access to the latest 45 rpm records. In addition, Mrs. Townsend always had snacks available.

I can remember sitting on his front screened in porch listening to those rock and roll records like it was yesterday. Several of us, Gail Snyder, Kandy Kelly, Martha Hayes, Susan Liles, Polly Byrd, Kate McMillian, Phillip Odom, Billy Posey, Jimmy Ezell, and Johnny Watson would rush to his house after school and listen to those "tunes' until dark.

The biggest treat of all occurred when Billy would play his guitar. At the age of eleven, I heard him play for the first time. He seemed to be able to play any song that was popular at that time. His version of "Party Doll" was my favorite. We talked, sang and learned to dance on that front porch. The tunes we listened to in those early days of 'Rock & Roll' were only the beginning of what was to come in the years ahead.

The 1950's gave birth to many new dance crazes. We had our version of the Jitterbug, plus the Bop, the Hand Jive, and the Stroll. Slow dancing at that time in our lives was very romantic, and we learned to do the Box step. Many of these were the dances performed by kids on American Bandstand.

American Bandstand was a Rock & Roll television show for teenagers produced in the North. I don't remember watching it until I was older, but our older friends saw the program and shared the latest dance steps with us. Rock & Roll music was making an impression on us and would have a great influence on our lives for years to come.

News of interest to us in 1956 and 1957

●Nikita Khrushchev said, "History is on our side. We will bury you!"

●President Eisenhower was re-elected

●Floyd Patterson knocked out Archie Moore to become the heavyweight champion of the world

●Don Larsen pitched the first "perfect" game in World Series history and the New York Yankees won the World Series

●On October and November, the Russians launched Sputnik I and Sputnik II. Sputnik II carried a live dog into space.

●The first U.S. civil rights bill since the *War Between The States* passed Congress and established a Civil Rights Commission which provided voting rights protection.

●President Eisenhower sent federal troops to Little Rock, Arkansas to control crowd demonstrations against integration.

●How the Grinch Stole Christmas was published by Dr. Seuss

●Barry Gordy, Jr. started *Motown Records* with $700.

●The Frisbee was an instant success

What I remember about 1956

Cost of living in 1956	
Gallon of Milk	97¢
Loaf of Bread	18¢
New Automobile	$2,100
Gallon of Gas	23¢
New Home	$22,000
Average Income	$4,454

Our favorite songs in 1956 included:

Blueberry Hill	**Fats Domino**
Devil Or Angel	**Clovers**
Don't Be Cruel	**Elvis Presley**
Graduation Day	**Four Freshmen**
Heartbreak Hotel	**Elvis Presley**
Hound Dog	**Elvis Presley**
In The Still Of The Night	**Five Satins**
Long Tall Sally	**Little Richard**
Love Me Tender	**Elvis Presley**

47

Journey of a Baby Boomer

Magic Touch (You've got)	**Platters**
My Prayer	**Platters**
Only You	**Platters**
See You Later Alligator	**Bill Haley/Comets**
Standing on the Corner	**Four Lads**
The Great Pretender	**Platters**
Tonight You Belong to Me	**Patience/Prudence**
Why Do Fools Fall In Love?	**Frankie Lymon**

What I remember about 1957

Cost of Living in 1957	
Gallon of Milk	$1.01
Loaf of Bread	19¢
New Automobile	$2,100
Gallon of Gas	24¢
New Home	$20,000
Average Income	$4,594

In 1957, the top songs were: "All Shook Up" performed by Elvis Presley; "Don't Forbid Me" sung by Pat Boone; as well as "Party Doll" by Buddy Knox. Also topping the musical charts that year were, "Wake Up Little Susie" by The Everly Brothers, "You Send Me" by Sam Cooke, and "Young Love" by Sonny James.

Our favorite songs of 1957 included:

A White Sport Coat & A Pink Carnation	Marty Robbins
All Shook Up	Elvis Presley
April Love	Pat Boone
At The Hop	Danny/The Juniors

Blue Monday	Fats Domino
Bye Bye Love	Everly Brothers
Chances Are	Johnny Mathis
Come Go With Me	Del-Vikings
Diana	Paul Anka
Every Day	Buddy Holly
Honeycomb	Jimmy Rodgers
I'm Walkin'	Fats Domino
It's Not For Me to Say	Johnny Mathis
Jailhouse Rock	Elvis Presley
Kisses Sweeter Than Wine	Jimmy Rodgers
Little Darlin'	Diamonds
Love Letters In The Sand	Pat Boone
Love Is Strange	Mickey & Sylvia
Party Doll	Buddy Knox
Peggy Sue	Buddy Holly
Silhouette	Rays
Teddy Bear	Elvis Presley
That'll Be The Day	Buddy Holly
Treat Me Nice	Elvis Presley
Twelfth Of Never	Johnny Mathis
Wake Up Little Susie	Everly Brothers

Age Of Innocence

Whole Lotta Shakin' Goin' On	**Jerry Lewis Lee**
You Send Me	**Sam Cooke**

News of interest to us in 1958

●The United States finally launched Explorer I, our first satellite

●Elvis Presley entered the United States Army

●An artificial sweetener known as Sweet n' Low could be bought in supermarkets

●The first Pizza Hut opened in Kansas City.

●Americans bought over 100 million Hula Hoops

●The New York Yankees beat Milwaukee in the World Series and the Brooklyn Dodgers moved to Los Angeles

What I remember about 1958

Cost of Living in 1958	
Gallon of Milk	$1.01
Loaf of Bread	19¢
New Automobile	$2,200
Gallon of Gas	24¢
New Home	$30,000
Average Income	$4,650

In 1958, the top songs were:"At the Hop" by Danny and The Juniors, "Bird Dog" by The Everly Brothers, "Don't" by Elvis Presley, "Get a Job" by The Silhouettes, "Sugartime" by McGuire Sisters; "Tequila" by The Champs, and "The Purple People Eater" by Sheb Wooley.

Our favorite songs of 1958 included:

26 Miles	**Four Preps**
All I Have To Do Is Dream	**Everly Brothers**
At The Hop	**Danny/The Juniors**
Book Of Love	**Monotones**

Journey of a Baby Boomer

Born Too Late	Poni-Tails
Chantilly Lace	Big Bopper
Do You Want to Dance	Bobby Freeman
For Your Precious Love	Jerry Butler
Get A Job	Silhouettes
Good Golly Miss Molly	Little Richard
Great Balls Of Fire	Jerry Lee Lewis
He's Got the Whole World	Lori London
I Wonder Why	Dion/The Belmonts
It's All In The Game	Tommy Edwards
It's So Easy	Buddy Holly
Johnny B. Goode	Chuck Berry
Maybe Baby	Buddy Holly
My Special Angel	Bobby Helms
Oh Boy	Buddy Holly
Purple People Eater	Sheb Wooley
Splish Splash	Bobby Darin
Summertime Blues	Eddie Cochran
Sweet Little Sixteen	Chuck Berry
Tears On My Pillow	Little Anthony
Tequila	Champs
To Know Him Is To Love Him	Teddy Bears

Age Of Innocence

Tom Dooley	**Kingston Trio**
Twilight Time	**Platters**
Who's Sorry Now?	**Connie Francis**
Witch Doctor	**David Seville**
Yakkety Yak	**Coasters**

My *Age of Innocence* centered around church, family and the home. I remember that we did things together as a family. We took trips, visited relatives, went to church as a family, ate meals together at the table, went on picnics and took Sunday afternoon rides.

My brothers and I played outside with the other kids until dark. I remember playing "Hide and Go Seek" with my friends at night. Our parents never worried about us being out after dark. On Saturdays, we didn't spend all day watching television, we spent as much time as possible outside with our friends. We weren't afraid of anything, except the wrath of our parents if we messed up. All the parents knew each other and all the kids. Gangs, gun violence and perverts were pretty much unknown to us.

Video games weren't around then, Transistor

radios were the "in thing" since Rock & Roll was cool. As much as I appreciate technology, the efforts of science to improve and prolong life, I often wish I could ***"Return to the thrilling days of yesteryear"***.

The Teenage Years

The 1960's brought about all types of change in the United States and around the world. John Fitzgerald Kennedy became the 35th president of the United States. It was President Kennedy's *"New Frontier"* campaign that inspired our nation, especially young people. The new President woke up the nation with his inaugural address by stating, "Ask not what your country can do for you. Ask what you can do for your country."

I heard words that were new to me, such as civil rights, segregation and integration. Today I hear more about gun control, metal detectors, police in schools, plus the need for more grief counselors and intervention specialists. There were love-ins, sit-ins, hippies, and flower children, but no terrorists in our schools. Many things were taking place around me that would affect me for the rest of my life.

During the 1960's new music sounds and dances erupted. I heard adults talking about Rock & Roll being the devil's music, saying that kids were going to end up in hell if they kept listening to that new stuff.

The Twist arrived on the scene as Chubby Checker made it a national and international sensation. We were moving and grooving with the new sound of Rock & Roll. I was able to do the Twist, proving it didn't take any special talent. After the Twist we were exposed to the Mashed Potato, the Hully Gully, the Madison and the Pony.

American Bandstand began as a local dance and musical talent show in Philadelphia. Over the years it was shown nationally and became more than a dance show. It introduced us to many major musical talents of the late fifties and early sixties. American Bandstand owed its success to Dick Clark. He turned a daily dance show into an national institution, and helped the careers of many singers and musicians along the way.

Much of the music expanded our vocabulary to include words our folks couldn't understand. The early 1960's were known as the era of "do wop" records. The songs included words and phrases such as "Sha-la-la-la", "Do-wop-do-wop", "Bee-bop-a-lula",

58

and "A-weem-a-wit, a weem-a-wit".

As teenagers we hung out at malt shops, drive-ins, drug stores, and bowling alleys. Sock hops, dances, and high school proms were part of our culture. Usually these were held in the school gym on the wooden basketball court or in the school cafeteria. Street shoes were forbidden on the gym floor, therefore the sock hop developed.

As teenagers our dress style was pretty simple. We wore shirts, slacks, tennis shoes, saddle oxfords, or penny loafers. Some of us wore watches, but ID bracelets were more popular. Girls wore their boy friend's class ring on a chain around their neck to indicate to the world that they were going steady with him. Often girls would wear the letter jacket of their boy friend which was a statement of the seriousness of the relationship.

Many of us wore our hair in crew cuts or flat tops and eventually added the duck tail. We went from short haircuts in the 50's to long sideburns and long hair. By my senior year most boys started wearing their hair in the short collegiate style. None of us would have thought about wearing an earring because we would have been laughed out of town. Later in the 1960's bell bottom pants for both girls and boys were popular.

Our Lifestyle

In the 1960's, "hanging out" was the thing for teenagers to do. We watched with envy as older friends drove cars and were able to cruise the drive-ins. We had no particular place to go, it was just the idea of being able to go if you had the chance. The guys that had won football letter jackets were our heroes and we looked forward to the day when we could establish ourselves on the gridiron.

It seemed that our day took forever to arrive. When our 16th birthday arrived, it was assumed that this was our day of freedom. No longer would we have to be taken places by our parents. A driver's license was a status symbol indicating that you had arrived.

I lived in El Paso when I turned 16 years old. That meant I was of legal age to get my driver's license. I had no trouble with the written part, but that parallel parking was a pain. One of life's most embarrassing experiences is when you fail to pass the driving test. The second time I took the test, I passed.

It was a thrill to be able to drive as a teenager, it meant you had finally arrived on the "grown-up" scene. Very few my age had their own car, but it seemed like they did. I remember using the family station wagon for my dates. Mom and Dad bought a 1959 Plymouth Station Wagon with automatic transmission, and the transmission was activated by pushbuttons. I would cruise the "Red Rooster" drive-in near Irvin High School hoping to see my friends to show off my new license.

Gypsy Days

Dad was an Army Officer and that meant he was reassigned about every two years to a different post. My family would pack up and actually look forward to the move and a new experience. It was difficult to leave friends and familiar surroundings, but as an Army family we adjusted quickly to our new home. Moving to a new Army post was like taking a vacation.

After the moving van packed our house hold items, Mom and Dad would pack the car for the trip. Packing the car was more involved in those pre minivan days. My parents had to pack our clothes and all necessary stuff in the trunk, then with our dogs in the back seat with me and my brothers the trip would begin.

There were no fast food places in those days so we ate at real restaurants. It was a treat to eat in a restaurant every night and be able to order stuff we never got at home. We stayed at roadside hotels or tourist courts, and the good ones had a TV in the room and a swimming pool out front.

I lived in the days before air conditioning, but in El Paso, Texas there were water cooling units on nearly every house to keep houses cool. The first automobile air conditioner I remember was our move from Fort Smith, Arkansas to El Paso in our 1954 Packard. What really stands out in my mind is traveling across Texas with our "air conditioner" attached to the passenger side window. It was a large metal cylinder mounted outside the passenger door which Dad filled with ice.

As he drove, air entered the cylinder, passed over the ice, then entered the car through the passenger window. Though it wasn't the most efficient unit by today's standards, we were able to travel across the Texas desert during the day. Several years passed before the automobile air conditioner was developed and became standard equipment on cars.

Our travels often took two or three days. There were no interstates and those two lane highways took us through small towns and big cities. Buddy, Doug and I would create games to play in the back seat. Each of us had our own side of the car and we protected our marked off territory. Often Mom would have to step in and referee situations that got out of hand and Dad would have to answer the question of the ages, "Daddy, how much longer before we get there?" Some things just haven't changed over the years.

I spent my teenage years in three great places, El Paso, Texas; Germany; and Brewton, Alabama.

Each place was special and still provides great memories.

Moving to Germany in 1963 from El Paso was a traumatic experience for me. I had my prized letterman's jacket, friends galore, a driver's license and a girlfriend. I felt secure in my world, but in January 1963 everything seemed to be coming apart. Moving meant leaving my friends at Irvin High School behind and beginning life all over.

When I arrived in Germany, I found things very different from the United States. First, very few teenagers drove automobiles. Teens walked everywhere and no one seemed to mind. Second, instead of cruising drive-ins we went to "Teen Clubs" where we would listen to all the latest records we could get our hands on, and to *BBC radio* which was transmitted from a ship off the coast of England. The *BBC* played the latest hits from all over the world, especially those of British groups.

I attended Kaiserslautern American High School with several hundred other "Army Brats", as we were known. Most of my new classmates saw living in Europe a dream come true and the opportunity of a lifetime. They had accepted their fate, but some of us only felt sorry for ourselves and made life miserable for our families. Some of us had a lot of growing up to do.

Television

Television viewing in the 1960's was totally different then today. The concept of television was different; we didn't plan our meals or activities around the programs. Today, television seems to take command of our lives and it is often turned on and may even run continuously even if nobody is watching it.

In the sixties, watching television was a special activity. We scheduled time for watching, and turned it on for specific shows. We just seemed to have more important things to do than become couch potatoes. Some of our favorites included westerns, comedies, adventures and programs that are known as sitcoms today.

During the sixties westerns such as Wagon Train, Bonanza, Gunsmoke, Rawhide, Branded, The Big Valley, The Rifleman, The Big Valley, and The Virginian received our viewing attention. Programs that centered on war themes were big for a few years. I remember watching Combat, Rat Patrol, 12 o'clock High, and my favorite Black Sheep Squadron.

When it came to comedies, Hazel, Red Skelton, Andy Griffith, Danny Thomas, My Three

65

Sons, The Real McCoys, Dennis The Menace, Gilligan's Island, My Favorite Martian, That Girl, Bewitched, The Lucy Show, Dobie Gillis, Gomer Pyle, Laugh-in, and The Smothers Brothers captivated us.

Detective drama and action adventures were very popular with us. As Baby Boomers we tuned in programs like Perry Mason, Ironside, The Fugitive, The FBI, 77 Sunset Strip, Adventures in Paradise, The Untouchables, The Man From UNCLE, The Mod Squad, Mission: Impossible, I Spy, Dragnet, and Batman. In addition, programs like Dr. Kildare and Ben Casey were popular with us.

T. R. Miller High School

I returned to Brewton, Alabama for my senior year of high school. I left Brewton after the 6th grade when Dad returned from Korea and had only returned there for periodic visits. Old friends from *my days of innocence* were my new classmates. It seemed as if I had never left. I immediately took my place as a member of the T. R. Miller High School family and my senior year proved to be exciting.

I enjoyed the small town flavor of Friday night football games and the parties afterwards. Often after home games someone would have a party. It was a time when we could get together, play records and enjoy each other's company. Saturday nights were spent at parties, the movies, creek banking, or cruising.

I spent many hours riding with friends up Douglas and Belleville Avenues. Our route would take us from the drive-in across from the Oaks Cafe to the bowling alley and back. In those days we could put $2.00 worth of gas in someone's car and ride around all night.

The bowling alley seemed to be the accepted meeting place for teenagers. We didn't actually bowl, but stood around outside and talked. If we stayed there long enough we would eventually see the entire senior class.

We had school dances and of course the annual Junior and Senior Prom. The theme for our prom was "Harbor Lights". The guys wore white jackets and our girl friends wore beautiful evening gowns. Other than graduation, the prom was the biggest event and most memorable of my senior year.

My senior class play was <u>The Night Of January 16th</u> by Ayn Rand. I had never been in a play before but was asked to play the part of Larry Regan, the gangster. The entire cast worked very hard and under the direction of Mrs. Rice played before a packed house at each nightly performance. I actually learned my part and had a great time doing the play.

Unsung Heroes

I was always fortunate to have wonderful teachers. I called them teachers, not educators, and their attitudes and love for teaching have had a profound influence on my life. Miller High School seemed to attract some of the finest teachers.

I took French my senior year. I had taken three years of Latin previously but wanted to become fluent in a living language. Mrs. Barbara Page was my teacher. I was the only 12th grader in the class and felt out of place at first. But Mrs. Page made me feel right at home. She was terrific and seemed to make that foreign language come to life.

Realizing I needed as much help as possible learning the language, she assigned me a seat between two of her best students, Patti Strain and Jimmy Reece. They tutored me, but eventually realized I was a lost cause when it came to learning French. I saw her a few years ago and she asked me *"Parlez-vous francais,?"*. I responded "not yet, but I'm still trying". Even the best teachers aren't able to teach some people.

My geometry teacher, Mrs. Becky (Barrett) Everage really knew her stuff. She was a no-nonsense teacher who expected the best from every pupil. She could explain those circles and pyramids in such a manner that they almost made sense to me. In addition to teaching, she was my guidance counselor. Becky, I can call her that now, was an encourager and gave me great advice that helped me during my undergraduate years.

Mrs. Julia Alice Rice taught my English class. She and her husband Norman meant a great deal to me that senior year so long ago. My classmates regarded them as the ideal couple. Coach Rice helped coach the football team and was the head baseball coach. Together they made an excellent team.

Mrs. Rice had the awesome task of teaching us our most dreaded subject. You could tell she loved the subject and wanted all of us to appreciate it as she did. It wasn't until years later that I finally saw what she meant about the power of literature on a person's life.

We had to write short papers about characters in Shakespeare's plays and read his works in class. I couldn't believe a guy that had been dead for centuries could make life so miserable for me. He just didn't make any sense at all to me. Now, after thirty years, I have finally learned to appreciate his work.

Mrs. Rice will always have a special place in my heart. In my high school year book the *"Tiger*

Roar" she wrote the following words next to her picture: *"To my overseas sweetheart-keep your goals high. You'll make it!"* The encouragement she and Coach Rice gave me in 1964 is the type needed by teenagers today who seem to be starving for attention and direction for their life.

Mason's Drug Store

Mason's Drug store was located at the intersection of Belleville Avenue and St. Joseph Street. The railroad tracks pass through the center of town and are only twenty-five feet from the drug store. In those days the railroads were very active with trains passing through Brewton on a regular basis. If you were in the drug store when trains passed through town, you could feel the building shake.

Mason's had the best hamburgers and chocolate milkshakes around. Although many people said the Oaks Cafe had better hamburgers, I liked Mason's. The soda fountain stools were pretty much occupied with teenagers during the hot summer days. We could order a fountain cherry Coke made with syrup and escape the humidity for a short time.

Mason's Drug Store no longer exists, having gone the way of many small town independent drug stores, but the building still stands today. A fine restaurant "Willie's Place" occupies the historic building. Each time I dine at Willie's, I am reminded of the good times we at Mason's.

Creek Banking

Friday and Saturday nights were often creek banking times. Along with our girlfriends we would head for the banks of Burnt Corn Creek. All it took was a little imagination to develop a party. We would build a bon fire, spread blankets on the sand, cook hot dogs, and enjoy our favorite beverages.

Transistor radios were a necessity. Anyone that had one was officially invited. We would sit around and listen to music, eat, gossip, sing and as the fire started to die down .....(you know what I mean).

The area was secluded and we pretty much had the run of the area. As I remember, the only problem we encountered was someone driving a car into the loose sand near the water. Although if the weather was warm, the crystal clear creek was a great place to swim at night.

The Death of Our President

John F. Kennedy was the 35th President of the United States. He was a young wealthy progressive senator from Massachusetts and a decorated World War II hero. His personality and innovative ideas gave our nation real hope of better things to come.

On November 22, 1963, I entered the gymnasium of T.R. Miller High School in Brewton, Alabama for physical education on that unforgettable day. Coach Jim Jefferies came into the gym with tears in his eyes and addressed the entire group. His voice cracked and he was almost speechless as he attempted to convey the news. His words caused a silence throughout the room that can't be described. Phillip Odom, Billy Townsend, Jimmy Ezell, Bill Hawk and I sat in disbelief as the tragic words echoed again and again throughout the vast building.

Young men and women cried that day, as a feeling of disbelief surrounded us like a tremendous dark cloud. I wondered how something like this could happen our great country. The effect of President Kennedy's untimely death left me in shock, but it was only the beginning of what was to come in the years ahead.

Our British Invasion

We had heard their music and seen their pictures but none of us had seen the *Beatles* perform. That was to end soon. The Ed Sullivan Show was going to give America the *Beatles* live on television. The broadcast was to take place on February 9, 1964. Nearly every teenager in Brewton, Alabama and across the nation waited faithfully for the day to arrive.

The program was scheduled for Sunday evening when most teenagers were expected to be in church. Ministers pleaded and warned us not to stay away from services in order to watch those long haired individuals from England. But, the requests did no good. At 7:00 P.M. on Sunday night, February 9, 1964, approximately 73 million young people crowded in front of televisions across America to get a glimpse of the new heroes of "Rock & Roll".

As in generations of the past music was a form of expression and identity for us. We had the music of Richie Valens, Jackie Wilson, Elvis, Fats Domino, the Silhouettes, the Platters, Danny and the Juniors, The Coasters, The Kingsmen, The Champs, Bo Diddley, The Big Bopper, Gene Chandler, Diana Ross and the Supremes, Otis Redding, Wilson Pickett, The Rascals, Aretha Franklin, The Four Tops, The Everly Brothers,

Buddy Holly, Gene Pitney, The Beachboys, Chubby Checker, Del Shannon, to name only a few and now the Beatles. The beat and words of the songs we embraced in the 1960's are part of our heritage. We danced, sang, drove, ate and slept to the music.

Little did I know that over thirty years after the Kingsmen made *Louie, Louie* popular it would be a party favorite of our children and used by marching bands at sporting events to excite crowds. Many of my favorites continue to be sung and listened to by our children.   Golden Oldie radio stations are more popular that ever.

News of interest to us in 1959

●Buddy Holly, Richie Valens, and the Big Bopper were killed in a plane crash near Clear Lake, Iowa

●The Nuclear submarine U. S. Nautilus traveled under the North Pole

●The Barbie doll was put on the market by Mattel

●Alaska and Hawaii became part of the United States

●Fidel Castro became the leader of Cuba

●The Los Angeles Dodgers won the World Series

What I remember about 1959

Cost of Living in 1959	
Gallon of Milk	$1.01
Loaf of Bread	20¢
New Automobile	$2,250
Gallon of Gas	25¢
New Home	$30,000
Average Income	$5,000

77

Our favorite songs of 1959 included:

In 1959, the top songs were: "A Big Hunk o' Love" by Elvis Presley; "Come Softly to Me" by Fleetwoods; "Dream Lover" by Bobby Darin; "Lonely Boy" by Paul Anka; "Mack the Knife" by Bobby Darin; "Stagger Lee" by Lloyd Price; "There Goes My Baby" by The Drifters; and "Venus" by Frankie Avalon.

Our favorite songs as teenagers in 1959 were numerous and included:

A Fool Such as I	Elvis Presley
A Teenager In Love	Dion & The Belmonts
Along Came Jones	Coasters
Beep Beep	Playmates
Bobby Socks To Stockings	Frankie Avalon
Charlie Brown	Coasters
Come Softly To Me	Fleetwoods
Dance With Me	Drifters
Donna	Richie Valens
Dream Lover	Bobby Darin
El Paso	Marty Robbins

I Only Have Eyes For You	Flamingos
La Bamba	Richie Valens
Lipstick On Your Collar	Connie Francis
Lonely Boy	Paul Anka
Lonely Teardrops	Jackie Wilson
Lonesome Town	Ricky Nelson
Love Potion No.9	Clovers
Mack The Knife	Bobby Darin
Misty	Johnny Mathis
Mr. Blue	Fleetwoods
Never Be Anyone Else But You	Ricky Nelson
Oh Carol	Neil Sedaka
Personality	Lloyd Price
Poison Ivy	Coasters
Primrose Lane	Jerry Wallace
Put Your Head On My Shoulder	Paul Anka
Sea Cruise	Frankie Ford
Sea of Love	Phil Phillips
Shout	Isley Brothers
Since I Don't Have You	Skyliners
Sixteen Candles	Crests
Stagger Lee	Lloyd Price

Journey of a Baby Boomer

The Battle Of New Orleans	**Johnny Horton**
The Happy Organ	**Dave Cortez**
There Goes My Baby	**Drifters**
Tijuana Jail	**Kingston Trio**
Till I Kissed You	**Everly Brothers**
Venus	**Frankie Avalon**

News of interest to us in 1960...

●Xerox introduced a paper copier

●The Russians shot down and captured Capt. Gary Powers when he flew a U-2 spy plane over Russia

●John F. Kennedy defeated Vice President Richard Nixon for President

●Soft drinks were available in aluminum cans for the first time

●Thomas S. Monaghan, started "Domino's" pizza with $500

●Chubby Checker introduced *The Twist* at the Peppermint Lounge in New York City

●The Pittsburgh Pirates defeated the New York Yankees to win the World Series

What I remember about 1960

Cost of Living in 1960	
Gallon of Milk	$1.04
Loaf of Bread	20¢
New Automobile	$2,275
Gallon of Gas	25¢
New Home	$30,000
Average Income	$5,200

Songs in 1960

In 1960, the top songs were: "Cathy's Clown" by The Everly Brothers; "El Paso" by Marty Robins; "I'm Sorry" by Brenda Lee; "Only the Lonely" by Roy Orbison; "Running Bear" by Johnny Preston; "Stuck on You" by Elvis Presley; "Teen Angel" by Mark Dinning; and "The Twist" by Chubby Checker.

We were 14 years old in 1960 and our favorite songs included:

Alley Oop	Hollywood Argyles
Are You Lonesome Tonight?	Elvis Presley
Cathy's Clown	Everly Brothers
Chain Gang	Sam Cooke
Corina, Corina	Ray Peterson
Devil Or Angel	Bobby Vee
Dreamin'	Johnny Burnette
Exodus	Ferante & Teicher
Georgia On My Mind	Ray Charles
I'm Sorry	Brenda Lee
It's Now Or Never	Elvis Presley

Itsy Bitsy Teenie Weenie Yellow Poka Dot Bikini	Brian Hyland
Last Date	Floyd Cramer
Let It Be Me	Everly Brothers
Let The Little Girl Dance	Billy Bland
Lonely Teenager	Dion
New Orleans	Gary U.S. Bonds
Only The Lonely	Roy Orbison
Puppy Love	Paul Anka
Running Bear	Johnny Preston
Save The Last Dance For Me	Drifters
Sixteen Reasons	Connie Stevens
Sweet Nothin's	Brenda Lee
Tell Laura I Love Her	Ray Peterson
The Twist	Chubby Checker
True Love Ways	Buddy Holly
Walk, Don't Run	Ventures
When Will I be Loved	Everly Brothers
Wild One	Bobby Rydell
You Got What it Takes	Marv Johnson
You Talk Too Much	Joe Jones
You're Sixteen, You're Beautiful	Johnny Burnette

News of interest to us in 1961...

●On April 12th, Russian cosmonaut Yuri Gagarin was the first man to travel into space. He traveled 187 miles above the earth for 90 minutes

●On May 5th America put a man in space. Navy Commander Alan B. Shepard, Jr., went for a 20 minute ride

●The Coca Cola company introduced Sprite

●Tylenol was introduced to consumers by Johnson & Johnson

●The Bay of Pigs invasion took place in Cuba

●East Germany closed the border between East and West Berlin and built the Berlin Wall

●President Kennedy created the Peace Corps

●The New York Yankees defeated Cincinnati and won the World Series

●Roger Maris hit 61 home runs and beat Babe Ruth's record of 60 home runs in a season

What I remember about 1961

Cost of Living in 1961	
Gallon of Milk	$1.05
Loaf of Bread	21¢
New Automobile	$2,275
Gallon of Gas	25¢
New Home	$30,000
Average Income	$4,315

Songs in 1961

In 1961, the top songs were: "Pony Time" by Chubby Checker; "Blue Moon" by The Marcels, "Hit The Road Jack" by Ray Charles, "Mother-In-Law" by Ernie K-Doe, "Surrender" by Elvis Presley, "Runaway" by Del Shannon, "Runaround Sue" by Dion, and "Please Mister Postman" by The Marvelettes.

We were 15 years old in 1961 and our favorite songs included:

A Hundred Pounds of Clay	Gene McDaniels
A Little Bit Of Soap	Jarmels
Big Bad John	Jimmy Dean
Blue Moon	Marcels
Briston Stomp	Dovells
Calendar Girl	Neil Sedaka
Can't Help Falling In Love	Elvis Presley
Crazy	Patsy Cline
Cryin'	Roy Orbison
Cupid	Sam Cooke
Dedicated To The One I Love	Shirelles
Every Beat Of My Heart	Gladys Knight
Goodbye Cruel World	James Darren
Hats Off To Larry	Del Shannon
Hello Mary Lou	Ricky Nelson
Hit The Road Jack	Ray Charles
I Fall To Pieces	Patsy Cline
I Love How You Love Me	Paris Sisters
Let's Twist Again	Chubby Checker

Mama Said	Shirelles
Michael (Row The Boat Ashore)	The Highwaymen
Moments To Remember	Lettermen
Moody River	Pat Boone
Moon River	Henry Mancini
Mother-In-Law	Ernie K-Doe
Peppermint Twist	Joey Dee/Starlighters
Please Mr. Postman	Marvelettes
Pony Time	Chubby Checker
Pretty Little Angel Eyes	Curtis Lee
Quarter To Three	Gary U. S. Bonds
Raindrops	Dee Clark
Rubber Ball	Bobby Vee
Run To Him	Bobby Vee
Runaround Sue	Dion /The Belmonts
Runaway	Del Shannon
Running Scared	Roy Orbison
Sad Movies Always Make Me Cry	Sue Thompson
School Is Out	Gary U. S. Bonds
Shop Around	Miracles
Spanish Harlem	Ben E. King
Stand By Me	Ben E. King

Take Good Care Of My Baby	Bobby Vee
The Lion Sleeps Tonight	Tokens
The Mountain's High	Dick & Dee Dee
The Way You Look Tonight	Lettermen
Tonight	Ferante & Teicher
Tossin' And Turnin'	Bobby Lewis
Tower of Strength	Gene McDaniels
Tragedy	Fleetwoods
Travelin' Man	Ricky Nelson
When I Fall in Love	Letterman
When We Get Married	Dreamlovers
Where The Boys Are	Connie Francis
Who Put The Bomp	Barry Mann
Will You Love Me Tomorrow	Shirelles

News of interest to us in 1962...

●*I got my Driver's License!*

●John Glenn circled the earth in Friendship 7, three times

●90% of Americans owned a television set and ABC began broadcasting in color

●Polaroid introduced color film which developed in 60 seconds

●The Cuban missile crisis occurred when Russia placed nuclear missiles in Cuba

●The Telstar I communications satellite was put in orbit

●The New York Yankees beat San Francisco and won the World Series

●Marilyn Monroe died from an overdose of sleeping pills

What I remember about 1962

Cost of Living in 1962	
Gallon of Milk	$1.04
Loaf of Bread	21¢
New Automobile	$2,275
Gallon of Gas	26¢
New Home	$30,000
Average Income	$5,500

In 1962, the top songs were: "Big Girls Don't Cry" by The Four Seasons; "Duke of Earl" by Gene Chandler; "Good Luck Charm" by Elvis Presley; "Johnny Angel" by Shelley Fabares, "Roses Are Red" by Bobby Vinton; "Sherry" by The Four Seasons; and "Soldier Boy" by The Shirelles.

We were 16 years old in 1962 and our favorite songs included:

409	Beach Boys
A Little Bitty Tear	Burl Ives
Ahab the Arab	Ray Stevens
Al Di La	Emilio Pericoli
All Alone Am I	Brenda Lee
Baby It's You	Shirelles
Beechwood 4-5789	Marvelettes
Big Girls Don't Cry	Four Seasons
Bobby's Girl	Marcie Blaine
Break It To Me Gently	Brenda Lee
Breaking Up Is Hard To Do	Neil Sedaka
Chip Chip	Gene McDaniels
Cryin' in the Rain	Everly Brothers
Dina	Johnny Mathis
Do You Love Me	Contours
Don't Hang Up	Orlons
Dream Baby	Roy Orbison
Duke Of Earl	Gene Chandler
Go Away Little Girl	Steve Lawrence

Green Onions	**Booker T & The MGs**
Happy Birthday Sweet Sixteen	**Neil Sedaka**
He's A Rebel	**Crystals**
Hey Baby	**Bruce Channel**
I Can't Stop Loving You	**Ray Charles**
I Remember You	**Frank Ifield**
If I Had A Hammer	**Peter, Paul & Mary**
Johnny Angel	**Shelley Fabares**
Johnny Get Angry	**Joannie Sommers**
Lemon Tree	**Peter, Paul & Mary**
Let's Dance	**Chris Montez**
Limbo Rock	**Chubby Checker**
Lonely Bull	**Herb Alpert**
Lover Please	**Clyde McPhatter**
Mashed Potato Time	**Dee Dee Sharp**
Monster Mash	**Bobby Pickett**
Next Door To An Angel	**Neil Sedaka**
Norman	**Sue Thompson**
Only Love Can Break A Heart	**Gene Pitney**
Palisades Park	**Freddy Cannon**
Papa Oom Mow Mow	**Rivingtons**
Party Lights	**Claudine Clark**

Teenage Years

Patches	Dickie Lee
Return To Sender	Elvis Presley
Roses are Red	Bobby Vinton
Sealed With A Kiss	Brian Hyland
She Cried	Jay/The Americans
Sheila	Tommy Roe
Sherry	Four Seasons
Shout	Joey Dee/Starlighters
Shout, Shout (Knock Yourself Out)	Erine Maresca
Soldier Boy	Shirelles
Stranger On The Shore	Mr. Acker Bilk
Surfin'	Beach Boys
Telstar	Tornadoes
The Loco-Motion	Little Eva
The Wah-Watusi	Orlons
The Wanderer	Dion/The Belmonts
Things	Bobbie Darin
Town Without Pity	Gene Pitney
Twistin' The Night Away	Sam Cooke
Unchain My Heart	Ray Charles
Venus In Blue Jeans	Jimmy Clanton
Where Have All The Flowers Gone	Kingston Trio

Journey of a Baby Boomer

Wolverton Mountain	**Claude King**
You Beat Me To The Punch	**Mary Wells**
You Don't Know Me	**Ray Charles**

News of interest to us in 1963...

●President Kennedy federalized the Alabama National Guard and ordered Gov. George C. Wallace to allow two black students to be enrolled at the University of Alabama

●Martin Luther King delivered his "I have a Dream" speech

●AT&T introduced touch-tone telephones

●President Kennedy was assassinated in Dallas, Texas

●New York's Idlewild Airport is named JFK Airport

●Dr. Michael DeBakey used an artificial heart to take over the functions of the heart during surgery

●President Kennedy visited Berlin and gave his "Ich bin ein Berliner" speech

●Pope John XXIII died and He was succeeded by Pope Paul VI

●The Supreme Court ruled that reading Bible verses in public schools was unconstitutional

●The Los Angeles Dodgers defeated the New York Yankees and won the World Series

What I remember about 1963

Cost of Living in 1963	
Gallon of Milk	$1.04
Loaf of Bread	21¢
New Automobile	$2,300
Gallon of Gas	25¢
New Home	$30,000
Average Income	$5,600

In 1963, the top songs were "Be My Baby" by The Ronettes; "Blowin' in the Wind" by Peter, Paul & Mary; "Easier Said Than Done" by Essex; "He's So Fine" by The Chiffons, "It's My Party" by Lesley Gore; "My Boyfriend's Back" by The Angels; "Walk Like a Man" by The Four Seasons; and "Walk Right In" by Rooftop Singers.

We were 17 years old in 1963 and our favorite songs included:

Down at Papa Joe's	Dixiebelles
Ain't That A Shame	Four Seasons
Another Saturday Night	Sam Cooke
Be My Baby	Ronettes
Be True To Your School	Beach Boys
Blowin' In The Wind	Peter/Paul & Mary
Blue On Blue	Bobby Vinton
Blue Velvet	Bobby Vinton
Busted	Ray Charles
Candy Girl	Four Seasons
Devil In Disguise	Elvis Presley
Do You Remember	Beach Boys
Don't Make Me Over	Dionne Warwick
Don't Say Nothing Bad About My Baby	The Cookies
Don't Think Twice It's Alright	Peter,Paul & Mary
Donna The Prima Donna	Dion & The Belmonts
Fools Rush In	Ricky Nelson
Forget Him	Bobby Rydell
Greenback Dollar	Kingston Trio

Half Heaven, Half Heartache	Gene Pitney
He's So Fine	Chiffons
Heat Wave	Martha Reeves
Hey Paula	Paul & Paula
I Will Follow Him	Little March Peggy
Wonder What She's Doing Tonight	Barry/Tamerlanes
I'm Leaving It All Up To You	Dale & Grace
If I Had A Hammer	Trini Lopez
In My Room	Beach Boys
It's My Party	Lesley Gore
It's Up to You	Ricky Nelson
Judy's Turn To Cry	Lesley Gore
Little Deuce Coupe	Beach Boys
Louie Louie	Kingsmen
Monkey Time	Major Lance
My Boyfriend's Back	Angels
On Broadway	Drifters
One Fine Day	Chiffons
Only In America	Jay & the Americans
Our Day Will Come	Ruby/Romantics
Popsicles & Icicles	Mermaids
Puff (The Magic Dragon)	Peter, Paul & Mary

Rhythm Of The Rain	Cascades
Ring of Fire	Johnny Cash
She's A Fool	Lesley Gore
Shout	Otis Day/The Knights
Sugar Shack	Jimmy Gilmer
Surfer Girl	Beach Boys
Surfin' U.S.A.	Beach Boys
The End of the World	Skeeter Davis
The Night Has A Thousand Eyes	Bobby Vee
Then He Kissed Me	Crystals
There I've Said it Again	Bobby Vinton
Two Faces Have I	Lou Christie
Up On The Roof	Drifters
Walk Like a Man	Four Seasons
Walk Right In	Rooftop Singers
Walking the Dog	Rufus Thomas
What Will My Mary Say	Johnny Mathis
Wipe Out	Safaris
You Can't Sit Down	Dovells
You Really Got A Hold On Me	Miracles
You're the Reason I'm Living	Bobby Darin

News of interest to us in 1964...

● We graduated from High School!

● President Johnson declared war on poverty

● Gasoline only cost 25¢ a gallon

● The G.I. Joe doll was introduced

● The poll tax was declared unconstitutional by the twenty-fourth amendment to the Constitution

● The Beatles appeared on the Ed Sullivan Show

● President Johnson signed the Medicare bill

● Brezhnev assumed power in the Soviet Union

● President Johnson announced an increase in United States aid to South Vietnam and Congress approved the Gulf of Tonkin Resolution

● Many of the Baby Boomer generation entered college

What I remember about 1964

Cost of Living in 1964	
Gallon of Milk	$1.06
Loaf of Bread	21¢
New Automobile	$2,350
Gallon of Gas	25¢
New Home	$30,000
Average Income	$5,880

Songs in 1964

In 1964, the top songs were: "Come See about Me" by The Supremes; "I Get Around" sung by The Beach Boys; "I Want to Hold Your Hand" by The Beatles; "Leader of the Pack" by The Shangra-Las; "Love Me Do" by The Beatles; "My Guy" by Mary Wells; and "The House Of The Rising Sun" by The Animals.

We were 18 years old in 1964 and our favorite songs included:

500 Miles	Peter, Paul & Mary
A Hard Day's Night	Beatles
A Summer Song	Chad & Jeremy
A World Without Love	Peter & Gordon
Abigail Beecher	Freddy Cannon
All I've Got To Do	Beatles
All My Lovin'	Beatles
And I Love Her	Beatles
Baby I Need Your Loving	Four Tops
Baby Love	Supremes
Bad To Me	Billy Joe Kramer
Because	Dave Clark Five
Big Man In Town	Four Seasons
Bits and Pieces	Dave Clark Five
Can't Buy Me Love	Beatles
Can't You See That She's Mine	Dave Clark Five
Chapel Of Love	Dixie Cups
Chug-A-Lug	Roger Miller
Come A Little Bit Closer	Jay/The Americans

Teenage Years

Come See About Me	Supremes
Dancing In The Street	Martha Reeves
Dang Me	Roger Miller
Dawn (Go Away)	Four Seasons
Dead Man's Curve	Jan & Dean
Do Wah Diddy Diddy	Manfred Mann
Do You Want To Dance	Del Shannon
Do You Want To Know A Secret	Beatles
Don't Let The Sun Catch You Crying	Gerry/Pacemakers
Everybody Loves Somebody	Dean Martin
Fun, Fun, Fun	Beach Boys
G.T.O.	Ronny/Daytonas
Glad All Over	Dave Clark Five
Goin' Out of My Head	Little Anthony
Hello Dolly	Louis Armstrong
Hey Little Cobra	Rip Chords
House of the Rising Sun	Animals
I Get Around	Beach Boys
I Only Want to be With You	Dusty Springfield
I Saw Her Standing There	Beatles
I Should Have Known Better	Beatles
I Want To Hold Your Hand	Beatles

I'm Happy Just To Dance With You	Beatles
I'm Into Something Good	Herman's Hermits
If I Fell In Love With You	Beatles
It Hurts To Be In Love	Gene Pitney
It's All Over Now	Rolling Stones
It's Over	Roy Orbison
Just Like Romeo & Juliet	Reflections
Leader Of The Pack	Shangri-Las
Little Children	Billy Joe Kramer
Little Honda	Beach Boys
Little Old Lady From Pasadena	Jan & Dean
Love Me Do	Beatles
Love Me with All Your Heart	Ray Charles Singers
Love Potion Number 9	Searchers
Maybelline	Johnny Rivers
Memphis	Johnny Rivers
Mountain of Love	Johnny Rivers
Mr. Lonely	Bobby Vinton
My Boy Lollipop	Millie Small
My Guy	Mary Wells
Navy Blue	Diane Renay
Needles And Pins	Searchers

Teenage Years

No Particular Place To Go	Chuck Berry
Oh, Pretty Woman	Roy Orbison
P.S. I Love You	Beatles
People Say	Dixie Cups
Please Mr. Postman	Beatles
Rag Doll	Four Seasons
Reach Out For Me	Dionne Warwick
Roll Over Beethoven	Beatles
Saturday Night At The Movies	Drifters
See The Funny Little Clown	Bobby Goldsboro
She Loves You	Beatles
She's A Woman	Beatles
She's Not There	The Zombies
Silence Is Golden	Four Seasons
Stay	Four Seasons
Suspicion	Terry Stafford
Tell Me Why	Beatles
It's In His Kiss	Betty Everett
The Way You Do The Things You Do	Temptations
There I've Said It Again	Bobby Vinton
Things We Said Today	Beatles
This Boy	Beatles

Time Is On My Side	**Rolling Stones**
Twist and Shout	**Beatles**
Under The Boardwalk	**Drifters**
Viva Las Vegas	**Elvis Presley**
Walk Don't Run	**Ventures**
Walk On By	**Dionne Warwick**
Walking In The Rain	**Ronettes**
We'll Sing In The Sunshine	**Gale Garnett**
Wendy	**Beach Boys**
When I Grow Up	**Beach Boys**
Where Did Our Love Go	**Supremes**
Wishin' and Hopin'	**Dusty Springfield**
You Can't Do That	**Beatles**
You Don't Have to be a Baby to Cry	**Caravelles**
You Don't Own Me	**Lesley Gore**
You Really Got Me	**Kinks**

When we were teenagers, we really didn't know how good our lives were. We had Rock & Roll, Drive-In's with Car Hops, Malt Shops, Drive-In Movies and we had our favorite Parking Spots, that no one else knew about. The teenagers of today will never experience the great times that we had.

My "Age of Innocence"

Anne's "Age of Innocence"

**Our Visit With Bertha in 1954.
(From Left) Me, Doug, Bertha & Buddy**

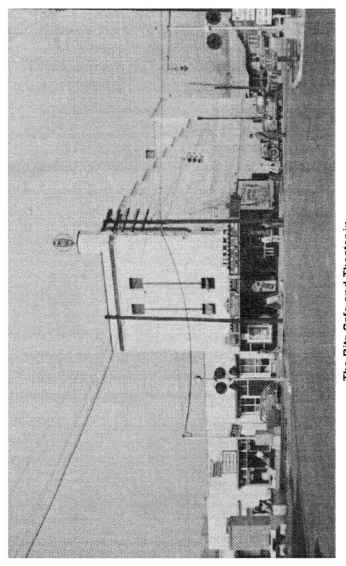

The Ritz Cafe and Theater in
Downtown Brewton, Alabama

Pappy Mitchell Plowing A Field In Scotts Hill, Tennessee in 1932

**My Grandparents, Pappy & Mamie Mitchell
in Scotts Hill, Tennessee 1934**

**My Daddy's Brothers & Sisters in 1934
Paul, Daddy, Henry, Lettie, Wesley and Lona**

The 1924 High School Graduation Picture
of Anne's Mother, Constance Saunders Bolton,
From Alma High School in Bayou La Batre, Alabama

Anne With Her Brothers, Charles
and Eddie, At A 1952 School Festival

My Mother and Father in the Fall of 1940

My Parents in 1942
Fred and Sybil Mitchell

113

Maw Maw, 1983

"The Choirboys" in Louisville, Kentucky, 1955
(From Left) Buddy, Me and Doug

**My Dad as Director of The Battleship Commission
During the 1980's
"The USS Alabama" in Mobile, Alabama**

Buddy and Dad With Governor Wallace in 1986.
Buddy was the Alabama Director of Finance
For Governor George C. Wallace in the 1980's.

My Brother Doug With Mom & Dad
On Christmas Day, 1990

T. R. Miller High School, Class of 1964
Brewton, Alabama

Some Members of My Platoon in December 1968

Christmas in Vietnam 1968

Near The Cambodian Border In December 1968

Doug, Ben and Jimmy
New Orleans 1996

90th Birthday Celebration Anne's Mother in Mobile, Alabama.
(From Left to Right) My Mother, Me, My Dad and Anne.
(Seated) Anne's Mother and Father

121

"Family Time in New Orleans 1996
Anne, Jim, Holly, Doug, Joy, Jimmy,
Amanda & Ben (Standing)

The College Years

The Loveliest Village on the Plains

In September 1964, I enrolled at Auburn University in Auburn, Alabama. I had spent the summer in Germany with my parents and returned to Alabama after my vacation to continue my education. I rode with Jimmy Ezell and Billy Posey to Auburn from Brewton in Billy's 1952 Ford. The old car wasn't much to look at, but it got us to where we were going.

There were no interstates in Alabama we could use at that time and the 200 mile trip on Highway 31 took us six hours. We traveled through towns like Evergreen, Georgiana, Greenville, Fort Deposit, Davenport, Pintlala, and Hope Hull before reaching Montgomery, then through Tuskegee before finally reaching Auburn.

Everything you needed, you could find in downtown Auburn. Most students didn't have cars and to get anywhere you had to walk. Freshmen were required to wear "Rat Hats" and participate in the

"Wreck Tech" parade wearing pajamas. Women had to live in the dorms on campus and were under strict curfews while in school. Those who didn't make their grades were placed on restriction by the dorm mother.

Women could not leave their dorms in shorts or slacks. Physical Education was mandatory and they had to wear shorts, therefore when they left their dorms they had to wear a raincoat so the men couldn't see their legs.

We wore coats and ties to football games and the women wore dresses and heels. Men purchased mums for their dates with either an "A" or fraternity Greek letters in the center. The corsage was adorned with orange and blue ribbons.

There were no fast food restaurants in Auburn in the mid 1960's. The closest thing we had to fast food was the *Kopper Kettle* and the *Tiger Cub*. *The Kopper Kettle* was open 24 hours and the only place you could get a quick hamburger. *The Sirloin Restaurant* was the place you took that special date. Toomer Drugs was the place to get a great glass of lemonade and you could cash checks for $1.00.

We went to football games, parties, played bridge, and rolled *Toomer's Corner* when we won football games away from home. The *War Eagle Supper Club, Plainsman,* and *Casino* were our stomping grounds. The *Plainsman* and *Casino* no longer exist, but the *War Eagle Supper Club* still thrives today for our children to experience.

My Fraternity Experience

During my first week on campus, I met men whose influence, example and friendship have had a tremendous impact my life. I was introduced to a group of fraternity men from Delta Tau Delta. Prior to that occasion I had not even considered becoming a member of a social fraternity.

I often think of the "good ole days" at the "Shelter" and the things that made my fraternity experience so great. It wasn't the Delt House, it was the men who made Delta Tau Delta so special. I learned about teamwork, organization, and responsibility. We were challenged to live up to the legacy left by outstanding alumni such as Ted Mallory, Phil Pauze', and Graham McDonald, Ken Mattingly, Paul Powers and others.

Wednesday night was reserved for chapter meeting, Thursday night was date night and Friday and Saturday nights we would have band parties. In 1967, I returned to Auburn to visit Anne and we went to a party at the Delt House. Rick Walker, one of my fraternity brothers, had a band and his band was playing that night. As soon as he saw me walk into the party with Anne, he dedicated a song to us that is still *"our song"* today. It was *When a Man Loves A Woman* by Percy Sledge. I have always felt that Rick did a better job with it than the original artist.

Many of the men in my fraternity were in R.O.T.C. and eventually served with honor in Vietnam. Mike Jeffries was my "Big Brother" and became a Marine pilot upon graduation. He was a great leader and very proud to be a Marine. He not only served with honor during the war, but also served his fraternity well. He would stand in front of the chapter and lead us in fraternity songs such as *"In Delta Hall", "The Night Patty Murphy Died",* and *"Take Down The Old Silver Goblet".*

There were many others that were part of my life during my college years like Benny Copeland, my first roommate. Wren Harper and his wife, Elaine, got me a blind date with Anne. Bert Ellis helped me with my first term paper and Tom Bohannon helped me with the new math.

I have great memories of my life at the shelter but I guess my most vivid are those of dinner time. It was customary for a brother to escort Annilee, our housemother, to dinner before anyone else could enter the dinning hall. I can still see James Chavers, Benny Robertson, Walt Schoditsch, Roger McClellan, Richard Reid, John Faulkner, Butch Lambert, Rick Alexander, James Brooks, Chris Old, Steve McQueen, Ron Dykes, John Harkins, and Tom Wright all attempting to escort Annilee Brown to the evening meal. They were being gentlemen but it also meant they would get to the dinner table before anyone else.

As I think back over the years, I remember those days at the shelter as a time of personal growth and fun. We had *black light* and *purple passion* parties without having to have police or security people monitor what was going on. We learned how to act like adults in addition to learning how to live and work with people from various backgrounds and economic statuses which has helped me throughout my life.

Panty Raids

During Spring Quarters in the exciting 60's, *Panty Raids* were the "in" thing. Wednesday nights seemed to be the appointed time. These events never accomplished anything and every male on the Auburn campus knew that. But it did seem to be a release of tension as the school year was nearing an end.

The raids would begin with as few as two dozen guys marching up Magnolia Avenue past fraternity row picking up volunteers prior to turning on Tiger Drive leading to the girl's dormitories. The noise was unbelievable as 3,000 mature college men walking as an organized group sang fraternity songs and prepared for an assault on the doors. (This assault meant standing outside the dorms and making fools of ourselves).

Rumors surfaced that the *Dean of Students*, Dr. James E. Foy and *Chief of University Police*, Dawson were nearby watching to ensure things didn't get out of hand. Supposedly these two had in their possession canisters of invisible paint to use in controlling the raid. Their aggressive attack could come at anytime and the paint could not be washed off and would show up on individuals for days after an application. The word spread that Dean Foy and Chief Dawson would visit fraternity houses the day after the raid took place with a special light that would locate participants sprayed with the special paint.

Of course, this put fear in the hearts of everyone, because that meant being kicked out of college. I don't think anyone participating in the raids ever saw what they hoped to see, but the camaraderie was fun. Oh, by the way, after thirty years, I want to put all those rumors to rest. I have asked Dean Foy about this so called invisible paint and his reply was "you never saw it, did you?"

The band parties, the hay rides, bon fires, parades, and parties provide exciting and lasting memories of the good ole days of college. Yes, we did attend classes and we had a library. In those days before computers and calculators we relied heavily on the *slide rule* to help get us through those math, chemistry and physics classes. Spring time in Auburn seemed to bring out the best in young college men.

Auburn Traditions

Some traditions and events have always been sacred to Auburn graduates. I remember some more vividly than others like, a fraternity brother getting thrown into the fish pool in front of Foy Union when he pinned a girl, celebrating a football victory at Toomers Corner, the *Burn the Bulldog parade*, and the *Wreck Tech parade*.

The Wreck Tech Parade

During the 1964 football season I was exposed to the Wreck Tech parade. Homecoming was special, but I had never experienced an event like that parade. The parade always took place prior to the Auburn-Georgia Tech football game. Fraternity and sorority pledges made floats that could be carried, wore "rat hats" and pajamas for the occasion.

Fraternities and Sororities worked on the floats all week. On Wednesday prior to the game it seemed

130

like the entire student body and town turned out for the event. The Auburn University marching band led the parade from the R.O.T.C. drill field up Magnolia Avenue to Toomers Corner, down Thach Avenue to the drill field. The streets were lined with thousands of people desiring to witness one of Auburn's great traditions.

Prior to the parade, with my "rat hat" on, I felt silly wearing my pajamas in public. But as the parade proceeded through town, I experienced a sense of pride as I participated in the event. This was an Auburn tradition and I was now part of it.

Auburn lost the game to Georgia Tech 7-3 in Atlanta. But Auburn played a great game and would have won except for a very controversial call by the officials at the end of the first half. Tucker Frederickson appeared to have scored a touchdown before the half ended, but the officials ruled he was down before crossing the goal line as time ran out.

Auburn played Georgia Tech for the last time on October 17, 1987. Anne and I, along with Wren and Elaine Harper made a special effort to be at the parade. Another Auburn tradition would be gone soon. As I watched the band and the students carrying floats parade by, I remembered my first "Wreck Tech" parade. When the last float passed down Thach Avenue I knew that something special to Auburn grads everywhere was now gone.

131

News of interest to us in 1965...

●In his State of the Union address, President Johnson proclaimed the "Great Society" program that was to eliminate poverty in the United States

●The Voting Rights Act became law

●The miniskirt became popular

●Diet Pepsi was available for the first time

●Malcolm X was assassinated

●Martin Luther King was arrested in Selma, Alabama

●Race riots broke out in the Watts section of Los Angeles

●The Grateful Dead became popular

●United States aircraft bombed North Vietnam

●Congress authorized the use of ground troops in Vietnam

●Antiwar rallies took place in the United States

●The Los Angeles Dodgers won the World Series

●Ralph Nader arrived on the scene and challenged the automobile industry safety standards

What I remember about 1965

Cost of Living in 1965	
Gallon of Milk	$1.05
Loaf of Bread	21¢
New Automobile	$2,350
Gallon of Gas	24¢
New Home	$40,000
Average Income	$5,940

In 1965, the top songs were: "Downtown" sung by Petula Clark, "Eight Days a Week" by The Beatles, "Help Me, Rhonda" by The Beach Boys, "I Got You Babe" by Sonny & Cher". Others were "I Hear a Symphony" by The Supremes, "My Girl" by The Temptations, "Stop! In the Name of Love" by The Supremes and "Ticket to Ride" by the Beatles.

We were 19 year old college freshmen in 1965 and the list of our favorite songs seemed to grow larger and larger.

1-2-3	Len Barry
A Taste of Honey	Herb Alpert
Act Naturally	Beatles
Ain't That Peculiar	Marvin Gaye
All I Really Want To Do	Sonny/Cher
Amen	Impressions
Any Way You Want It	Dave Clark Five
Baby Don't Go	Sonny/Cher
Baby I'm Yours	Barbara Lewis
Baby It's You	Beatles
Baby The Rain Must Fall	Glenn Yarbrough
Back In My Arms Again	Supremes
Bye, Bye, Baby (Baby Goodbye)	Four Seasons
California Girls	Beach Boys
Cara Mia	Jay/The Americans
Catch Us If You Can	Dave Clark Five
Crying In The Chapel	Elvis Presley
Do You Believe In Magic	Lovin' Spoonful

Do You Wanna Dance?	Beach Boys
Don't Think Twice	Wonder Who
Down In The Boondocks	Billy Joe Royal
Downtown	Petula Clark
Ebb Tide	Righteous Brothers
Eight Days A Week	Beatles
England Swings	Roger Miller
Everybody Loves A Clown	Gary Lewis/Playboys
For Your Love	Yardbirds
Get Off Of My Cloud	Rolling Stones
Hang On Sloopy	McCoys
Help Me Rhonda	Beach Boys
Help	Beatles
Hold Me, Thrill Me, Kiss Me	Mel Carter
How Sweet It Is (to be loved by you)	Marvin Gaye
Hurt So Bad	Little Anthony
I Can't Help Myself	Four Tops
I Go To Pieces	Peter/Gordon
I Got You Babe	Sonny & Cher
I Hear A Symphony	Supremes
I Knew You When	Billy Joe Royal
I Know A Place	Petula Clark

I Like It Like That	Dave Clark Five
I'll Be Doggone	Marvin Gaye
I'll Follow The Sun	Beatles
I'll Never Find Another You	Seekers
I'm A Man	Yardbirds
I'm Henry VIII, I Am	Herman's Hermits
I'm Telling You Now	Freddie/Dreamers
It Ain't Me Babe	The Turtles
It's Not Unusual	Tom Jones
Keep On Dancing	Gentrys
King Of The Road	Roger Miller
Let's Hang On	Four Seasons
Like a Rolling Stone	Bob Dylan
Make Me Your Baby	Barbara Lewis
Make the World Go Away	Eddie Arnold
Mr. Tambourine Man	Byrds
Mrs. Brown You've Got A Lovely Daughter	Herman's Hermits
My Girl	Temptations
Nothing But Heartaches	Supremes
Nowhere To Run	Martha Reeves
Papa's Got A Brand New Bag	James Brown
Rescue Me	Fontella Bass

College Years

Satisfaction	Rolling Stones
Save Your Heart For Me	Gary Lewis
Seventh Son	Johnny Rivers
Sounds of Silence	Simon /Garfunkel
Stop! In The Name Of Love	Supremes
Tell Her No	The Zombies
The Birds And The Bees	Jewel Akens
The Boy From New York City	Ad Libs
The In Crowd	Dobie Gray
The Name Game	Shirley Ellis
The Tracks Of My Tears	Smokey Robinson
This Diamond Ring	Gary Lewis
Ticket To Ride	Beatles
Turn! Turn! Turn!	Byrds
Unchained Melody	Righteous Brothers
Under My Thumb	Rolling Stones
We Can Work It Out	Beatles
We Gotta Get Out Of This Place	Animals
What The World Needs Now Is Love	Jackie DeShannon
What's New Pussycat	Tom Jones
Willow Weep for Me	Chad & Jeremy
Wonderful World	Herman's Hermits

Journey of a Baby Boomer

Wooly Bully	**Sam The Sham**
Yes I'm Ready	**Barbara Mason**
Yesterday	**Beatles**
You're Gonna Lose That Girl	**Beatles**
You've Got Your Troubles	**Fortunes**
You've Lost That Lovin' Feelin'	**Righteous Brothers**

News of interest to us in 1966...

●The war in Vietnam began to escalate

●Proctor & Gamble marketed Pampers for the first time

●Race riots broke out in Atlanta and Cleveland

●The Supreme Court issued the "Miranda" ruling

●The Baltimore Orioles won the World Series

What I remember about 1966

Cost of Living in 1966	
Gallon of Milk	$1.11
Loaf of Bread	22¢
New Automobile	$2,410
Gallon of Gas	23¢
New Home	$40,000
Average Income	$6,000

In 1966 the top songs were: "Good Lovin" by The Young Rascals, "My Love" sung by Petula Clark,"Paint It Black" by The Rolling Stones, "Summer in the City" by The Lovin' Spoonful, "We Can Work It Out" by The Beatles and my favorite, "When a Man Loves a Woman" by Percy Sledge.

139

We were 20 year old college sophomores in 1966, many were worried about *draft deferments* as Vietnam heated up, but we still listened to our music.

19th Nervous Breakdown	**Rolling Stones**
634-5789	**Wilson Picket**
A Groovy Kind Of Love	**Wayne Fontana**
Ain't Too Proud To Beg	**Temptations**
Along Comes Mary	**Association**
As Tears Go By	**Rolling Stones**
Ballad Of The Green Beret	**Sgt. Barry Sadler**
Bang Bang (My Baby Shot Me Down)	**Cher**
Barbara Ann	**Beach Boys**
Barefootin'	**Robert Parker**
Black Is Black	**Los Bravos**
Born a Woman	**Sandy Posey**
California Dreaming	**Mamas & Papas**
Cherish	**Association**
Cherry Cherry	**Neil Diamond**
Day Tripper	**Beatles**
Devil With The Blue Dress	**Mitch Ryder**

College Years

Song	Artist
Did You Ever Have To Make Up Your Mind	Lovin' Spoonful
Don't Bring Me Down	Animals
Don't Mess with Bill	Marvelettes
Double Shot Of My Baby's Love	Swingin' Medallions
Eleanor Rigby	Beatles
Five O'Clock World	The Vogues
Flowers on the Wall	Statler Brothers
Get Ready	Temptations
God Only Knows	Beach Boys
Good Day Sunshine	Beatles
Good Lovin'	Rascals
Good Vibrations	Beach Boys
I Can't Help Falling in Love With You	Elvis Presley
I Couldn't Live Without Your Love	Petula Clark
I Fought The Law	Bobby Fuller
I Got You (I Feel Good)	James Brown
I Saw Her Again	Mamas & Papas
I'm A Believer	Monkees
I'm So Lonesome I Could Cry	B. J. Thomas
I've Got You Under My Skin	Four Seasons
Kicks	Paul Revere/Raiders
Lady Godiva	Peter & Gordon

Last Train To Clarksville	Monkees
Lightnin' Strikes	Lou Christie
Listen People	Herman's Hermits
Little Red Riding Hood	Sam The Sham
Look Through Any Window	Hollies
Love Is Like An Itching In My Heart	Supremes
Love is a Hurtin' Thing	Lou Rawls
Mellow Yellow	Donovan
Monday, Monday	Mamas & Papas
Mustang Sally	Wilson Pickett
My Love	Petula Clark
My World Is Empty Without You	Supremes
Oh How Happy	Shades of Blue
Don't You Worry 'Bout Me	Four Seasons
Paint It Black	Rolling Stones
Paperback Writer	Beatles
Rain on the Roof	Lovin' Spoonful
Reach Out I'll Be There	Four Tops
Red Rubber Ball	Cyrkle
Rhapsody In The Rain	Lou Christie
See You In September	Happenings
She's Just My Style	Gary Lewis

Snoopy vs The Red Baron	Royal Guardsmen
So Lonesome I Could Cry	B.J. Thomas
Solitary Man	Neil Diamond
Somewhere, My Love	Ray Conniff
Soul And Inspiration	Righteous Brothers
Summer In The City	Lovin' Spoonful
Summertime	Billy Stewart
Sunny	Bobby Hebb
Sunshine Superman	Donovan
The Dangling Conversation	Simon/Garfunkel
The More I See You	Chris Montez
Sun Ain't Gonna' Shine Any More	Walker Brothers
This Door Swings Both Ways	Herman's Hermits
Time Won't Let Me	Outsiders
Trains and Boats and Planes	Dionne Warwick
Uptight	Stevie Wonder
What Becomes of the Broken Hearted?	Jimmy Ruffin
What Now My Love	Sonny & Cher
When A Man Loves A Woman	Percy Sledge
Where Were You When I Needed You	Grassroots
Wild Thing	The Troggs
Winchester Cathedral	New Vaudeville

Journey of a Baby Boomer

Workin' in a Coal Mine	Lee Dorsey
Working My Way Back To You	Four Seasons
Wouldn't It Be Nice	Beach Boys
Yellow Submarine	Beatles
You Can't Hurry Love	Supremes
You Didn't Have To Be So Nice	Lovin' Spoonful
You Don't Have To Say You Love Me	Dusty Springfield
You Keep Me Hangin' On	Supremes

The War Of Our Generation

There was a war in a southeast Asian country called Vietnam. Many were asking questions such as: What is the war all about? Why do we have to send Americans over there to die? Many questions were raised about this war, but very few answers seemed to satisfy Americans, especially young people. Many my age protested and demonstrated, and some burned their draft cards and our sacred American Flag. The cry heard across the nation was: "Make Love Not War."

The War in Vietnam was different from all other wars in which the United States has been involved. The average age of a soldier was 19, while the average in World War II was 26. During the Vietnam War many went to college to avoid going to war. Often men had to explain why they fought in the war, when not

145

serving was acceptable.

Soldiers served a tour of duty, normally one year. Men usually went to Southeast Asia individually and joined a unit when they arrived in country. In previous wars men went to the combat area as a member of an established unit. There was little support for the combat soldier or the war from the overall population of the United States.

The war was fought in a country that had not threatened our country and whose religion, history, culture, and values were very different from ours. In combat, soldiers found no front lines and there was no rear area, the entire country was a battle zone. The goal of the war was not clear, and America never indicated that she would do whatever was necessary to win. Territory was taken, lost, and taken again at the cost of more lives lost in combat than fighting casualties in World War II.

Soldiers returned home to America as individuals, not as a member of a unit as often took place in other wars. We were often met with insults, sneers, and disrespect after giving up a year of our lives to obey the orders of our country. There was no emotional support offered to soldiers fortunate enough to return home except for that of family and some friends.

For the most part soldiers returning from combat were turned out by *Uncle Sam* into a hostile society that did not recognize or appreciate their sacrifice. No war since *The War Between The States* caused such a rift in American public opinion which led to civil and social unrest and violence within our own country.

My *Patriotic Spirit*

In 1966 I made the decision to leave college and join the Army. I felt at the time it was the correct action for me to take. I had always liked the Army and had aspirations of making the Army my career just as my Dad had done. I went home to Ft. Benning, Georgia, and told Mom and Dad my plans.

They thought it was a good idea, except for the timing. The United States was getting more deeply involved in Vietnam everyday and my chances of going over to the war in Southeast Asia would be great. Dad wanted me to get into an area of training that I could utilize when I got out. I knew he was right and I listened to his advice.

The next day I went to see an Army recruiter to sign up. The recruiter told me about all the opportunities available to me. I saw slide shows, film strips and read about every program the Army had to offer. I made my decision and signed up.

When I returned home that night, I told Mom and Dad that I had made my decision and had signed up. Dad said, "Son, I bet you decided to enter the medical corps and become a medical technician so you can get a good paying job when you get out of the

Army". I said, "No, Dad, that's not the branch I selected".

Dad said, "Well then, you must have selected the field of law and decided to go into the area of law administration". I said, "No, Dad, that's not right either. I decided to enlist in the Airborne Infantry and go to Officer Candidate School." You could have knocked my dad (a career Infantry Officer) over with a feather. His only words were, "That's real good, son. There must be thousands of organizations that will be glad to hire an individual that learned how to jump out of perfectly good airplanes." Seriously, I know Dad was proud of me for selecting the Infantry and following in his footsteps.

When I went to "jump school" and later assigned to the 82nd Airborne Division after Officer Candidate School, Dad was in Vietnam. Making parachute jumps out of choppers, C-130's and C-140's was fun, but to this day I can't believe I actually jumped out of perfectly good airplanes.

My War

My orders for Vietnam came when I least expected. My father had volunteered for combat hoping that I would not have to serve, since two in the same family were not sent into a war zone at the same time. But within a few months after he returned, I was notified to report to Vietnam.

I left the comfort and love of my family to serve my tour. Anne and I found out just prior to my departure that we would become parents while I was gone. Our excitement about the impending birth was overshadowed by our upcoming separation. This was truly going to be rough year for both of us.

In 1968, as a young Lieutenant in the United States Army, I arrived in Vietnam. The time spent learning how to be a leader with the 82nd Airborne Division at Ft. Bragg, North Carolina, helped build up my confidence and partially prepared me for the year ahead.

When Dad returned from Vietnam a few months prior to my departure, the guidance and advice he gave helped prepare me. But no training or advice from those who had served in Vietnam could prepare me for what the next year of my life would be like.

I grew up fast! Within days my new home, with

the 25th Infantry Division located in Tay Ninh proved to be more than I expected. I'll never forget the smell of the banana groves, the sight of Nui Bau Den rising 2,700 feet high above the rice paddies, the Cao Dai Temple riveted with bullet holes, and the small innocent children caught in a war they didn't create.

It didn't take long to receive my *Baptism by Fire*. My second day out as a platoon leader our company was ambushed and the mountain *Nui Bau Den*, known as *the Black Virgin Mountain*, became a source of fear for me. I'll carry with me forever the sight of young men who were killed that September day. They had obeyed the orders of their country to help fight aggression in a far country and given all anyone could ask, their lives.

That night, I had to write letters home to the wives and parents of the three young men killed from my platoon that day. To this day, it was the most difficult thing I have ever had to do. I prayed that my commanding officer wouldn't have to write my family in the future.

The Wall

I very seldom talked about the war after returning from Vietnam. Each day the memories of that year clouded my mind with fear and hurt. It wasn't until a minister friend of mine, Tom Denton, helped me deal with the demons of fear, hate and sorrow that I was actually able to discuss my experience with anyone.

In 1994, Anne and I went to Washington, D.C. for the National Speakers Association Annual convention. While there, we went to the "Vietnam Memorial". She held my hand and together we walked down the path that lead to the "Wall". Just visiting and touching the "Wall" will grab your heart. I saw the names of brave men in I had known etched in the stone. Men who had so much to live for and so much to offer were gone. I couldn't hold back the tears, and I cried.

I remember many of my comrades in arms of the 25th Infantry Division who died in the war such as:

Albert Butler, Lieutenant Colonel

Ronald Matel, 1st Lieutenant

Duane Landwehr, 2nd Lieutenant

John Inguillo, Staff Sergeant

Larry Gosh, Sergeant

John Hughes, Sergeant

Bruce Mynard, Sergeant

Norman Teeter, Sergeant

Richard Cyran, Specialist 4

Richard Randolph, Specialist 4

James Clark, Private First Class

Bob Essman, Private First Class

Carl Lynch, Private First Class

Dennis Manson, Private First Class

Steve McCloud, Private First Class

John Rhodes, Private First Class

Richard Valadez, Private First Class

My home town of Brewton, Alabama and her sister town across the creek of East Brewton were touched several times by the untimely deaths of her young men. I often think of the friends I had known most of my life who did not return from Vietnam and the impact their lives might have made.

United States Army

William Richard Ellis, Staff Sergeant

Charles Donnette Gipson, Staff Sergeant

Joseph Earl Hammac, Specialist 4

James Floyd Madden, Corporal

Johnson Marcus Milligan, Warrant Officer

Obie Clyde Simmons, Private First Class

Donald Wayne Smith, Specialist 4

JC Summerlin, Specialist 4

Jimmy Ray Thomas, Private First Class

United State Marines Corps

David Marshall Haveard, Lance Corporal

Dalton Buster Lowery, Lance Corporal

John Wesley Winter, Corporal

I honor these men, some I knew and others I wish I had taken the time to get to know. You can find their names in places of honor on the Vietnam Wall in Washington, D.C. As a country, we will never know what they might have contributed to the future of our great nation.

The Ambush

Captain Carl Smith was my company's artillery liaison officer. He was a graduate of the University of Alabama and I had Auburn University blood. Even in the midst of battle the two of us had an on going friendly feud.

On the eve of the 1968 Auburn vs. Alabama game, I was to take an ambush patrol to the base of Nui Bau Den (The Black Virgin Mountain). Our battalion intelligence indicated that a company of Viet Cong would come down the mountain that night to attack our fire support base. We were ordered to maintain strict radio silence.

We established our ambush position, called in our location to the fire support base and waited in total silence for the enemy to cross our path. Around 2 AM radio silence was broken when a quiet voice came across my radio that announced, "Crimson 24, Y'all 16." Fortunately for my platoon our position was not compromised by the communication.

Just prior to dawn we received orders to abandon the ambush and return to base camp. When we passed through the concertina wire that surrounded the fire support base, I was greeted by a big sign which read,

"The Crimson Tide 24-Tigers 16"
That's 10 in a row Lt. Mitchell

The next year, 1969, Auburn University defeated Alabama 49-26, ending ten years of Crimson Tide dominance. I was unable to get in contact with Captain Smith to express my condolences.

Christmas In A Far Country

December, 1968-The past several weeks had been rough for the entire battalion. We had been in several fire fights and taken many casualties in addition to the constant harassment at night from enemy mortar fire.

On December 15th (which happened to be my father's birthday), we were ambushed by a battalion of North Vietnamese Regulars in an area near the Cambodian border. The small arms fire and incoming mortar fire were the worst I have ever experienced. The battle lasted from early morning to near dark before we were able to gain an upper hand and evacuate our casualties.

Needless to say, those of us who survived the day and the month were down both physically and emotionally. It was lonesome enough to be away from your family during the holiday season but the recent events made it even worse. Combat soldiers of past wars, separated from family and friends, have also experienced depression and homesickness at this special time, and it looked like Christmas 1968 was to be the worst I would ever remember.

My company had set up a small fire support base between Nui Bau Den and an old French Fort. This was a major infiltration route of the North Vietnamese Army from Cambodia to South Vietnam.

Our orders were to search out the enemy and stop them from reaching Tay Nihn City and Saigon.

Christmas Day 1968 gave all of us the hope that it would be quiet and uneventful. The family of one of my men had sent him an artificial Christmas tree. As we gathered around his bunker and told stories of home surrounding Christmas Day, I suddenly noticed the empty claymore mine box on which the tree was sitting. There was an imprint on the side of the pine box which I had not noticed in the past. It read:

T. R. Miller Mill Company
Brewton, Alabama

I had trouble believing what I was seeing. Brewton, Alabama was my hometown, I graduated from T. R. Miller High School and the T. R. Miller Mill Company was owned by old friends, the McMillian and Miller families.

I was so excited about my discovery that I sent a picture to the local newspaper with the following note: "Although I'm a long way from home today, this box of claymore mines brought a little joy to me. As you can see, it was made at T.R. Miller Mill Co. in Brewton. Needless to say, I was surprised to see it. The name of Brewton can be found in nearly every outpost, Fire Support Base, or what have you, in Vietnam. Once again, Merry Christmas and happy holidays."

Christmas Day over the years has provided me with some wonderful memories. But Christmas 1968 will always be remembered as very special because of my chance encounter with a wooden ammo box from my home town.

My First Father's Day

In May 1969, I received a radio message while in the field that Anne had given birth to my son. He was born on May 12th and she named him James Fred Mitchell, III but he would be called Jimmy. I was so proud to be a father, but more proud of Anne for her strength and courage. They say that "distance makes the heart grow fonder" and I believe it to this day.

Shortly after Jimmy was born I received a letter from my mother. She wrote, *"I truly believe your marriage was made in heaven! You should be very proud of Anne."* I had been praying daily that God would allow me to return home to her, and now I had another reason, Jimmy. After all, if our marriage was made in heaven that was the only possible outcome. Plus, my mother is never wrong.

God blessed me and answered my prayers, for I returned home from Vietnam on July 13, 1969. I was met at the airport in Mobile, Alabama, by my family and Anne's family. They were all there, and each moment of fear I had experienced the past year seemed to have vanished because I was with my family once again. This was the moment I had lived for and they were there to share it with me.

161

I remember walking down the steps of the aircraft and surveying the crowd. I saw Anne immediately and in her arms was my two month old son. My prayers had been answered, I was home. I held Jimmy in my arms, he scratched himself on my uniform ribbons and he cried. Anne seemed to know that I was afraid of him and took him in her arms, as only a mother can do, and he quit crying.

Vietnam had taken a year away from us. We could not bring back those lost days, but we could live for tomorrow. The love we had for each other before the war had grown stronger and we were ready to begin our life together as God had intended.

Prayer Of The French Paratrooper
(Author Unknown)

Give me, my Lord, that which you have left over.

Give me that which you are never asked for.

I do not ask for wealth, nor for success, nor even for health.

You are asked so often for this, my Lord, that you must not have any left.

Give me, my Lord, for which you are never asked.

Give me that which others refuse to accept.

I want insecurity and restlessness, I want torment and strife and that you should give them to me, my God, once and for all.

Let me be sure to have them always,

For I will not always have the courage to ask for them.

When I arrived at Ft. Bragg, North Carolina in October 1967, I was assigned to the 2/504, of the 82nd Airborne Division. The battalion nickname was *"The Devils In Baggy Pants"*. This was given to them by the Germans in World War II. It was a proud outfit

163

and I was excited about the assignment. All new officers assigned to the unit received an initiation and indoctrination. I received a copy of this poem at that time.

On Christmas 1966, Mother and Dad gave me a small pocket Bible that I carried with me every day while in Vietnam. Inside the cover, I had the poem which I would read from time to time. It was a reminder to me to always ask God for courage and strength each day.

The Moon Walk

On July 9, 1969, I arrived at the 90th Replacement Detachment at Long Binn, for my return to the United States. My flight from Bien Hoa Air Force Base the next day was called the "Freedom Bird". I spent most of my remaining time in *'the land I will never forget'* as close to a bunker as I could. I had made it this far and with one day to go, I was not going to take any chances. I looked at the faces of hundreds of men who were just arriving in "the Nam" and silently prayed they would also return home one day.

The next day I got on the "Freedom Bird" and started the long flight home. Everyone on board the aircraft with me sat in silence. Then the pilot announced that we were leaving Vietnam airspace and the cheering, excitement and singing filled the once quiet *"bird"*. We landed many hours later at Travis Air Force Base in California and were taken to the Oakland Army Terminal for debriefing and discharge.

Once I went through out-processing, I went to the San Francisco Airport for the flight to Mobile, Alabama. I really wasn't prepared for what I saw. Many changes were taking place in my country. I had been isolated from the political unrest, riots, and protests by people my age that captured the attention of the news media and the nation.

165

My biggest surprise would take place a few days after I returned home. The United States was scheduled to land astronauts from Apollo 11 on the moon. Television would televise the event. On July 20th, astronaut Neil Armstrong took mankind's first step on the moon as Anne and I along with millions of Americans watched the historic event live on television.

After a four day trip from the surface of the Earth, Neil Armstrong's words **"Houston, Tranquility Base here. The *Eagle* has landed"** sent chills through my body and once again made me proud to be an American.

Approximately six hours later after stepping on the surface of the moon, his words **"That's one small step for man, one giant leap for mankind"** briefly took my mind away from the war I had only days before left behind. This historic event made the horrible taste of war, death and destruction seem very far away for a brief time.

News of interest to us in 1967...

●The Green Bay Packers defeated the Kansas City Chiefs in the first Super Bowl

●The first compact microwave oven for the home was called the Radar-Range

●Israel won The Six-Day War over Syria and Egypt

●Race riots in Detroit killed 43 people and in Newark, New Jersey 26 people were killed

●The St. Louis Cardinals beat the Boston Red Sox to win the World Series

●Anti-war demonstrations broke out in Chicago, Philadelphia, Los Angeles, Oakland and at the Pentagon

●"Rolling Stone Magazine" began publication

●The World Boxing Association took away Muhammad Ali's title because he refused to enter the military

●Dr. Christian Barnard performed the world's first heart transplant in South Africa

What I remember about 1967

Cost of Living in 1967	
Gallon of Milk	$1.15
Loaf of Bread	22¢
New Automobile	$2,435
Gallon of Gas	28¢
New Home	$40,000
Average Income	$6,120

In 1967 the top songs were "Daydream Believer" by the Monkees, "Happy Together" by The Turtles, "Light My Fire" by the Doors, and "Penny Lane" by The Beatles.

I was 21 years old and in the Army when many of my friends were college Juniors in 1967 and our favorite songs included:

I'm Not Your Stepping Stone	**Monkees**
A Natural Woman	**Aretha Franklin**
A Whiter Shade Of Pale	**Procol Harum**
Alfie	**Dionne Warwick**

168

War Years

All You Need Is Love	Beatles
Apples, Peaches, Pumpkin Pie	Jay/Techniques
At The Zoo	Simon /Garfunkel
Bend Me Shape Me	American Breed
Brown-Eyed Girl	Van Morrison
By The Time I Get To Phoenix	Glen Campbell
C'mon Marianne	Four Seasons
Can't Take My Eyes Off of You	Frankie Valli
Carrie Anne	Hollies
Come Back When You Grow Up Girl	Bobby Vee
Daydream Believer	Monkees
Dedicated To The One I Love	Mamas & Papas
Funky Broadway	Wilson Pickett
Georgy Girl	Seekers
Girl You'll Be A Woman Soon	Neil Diamond
Groovin	Rascals
Happy Together	The Turtles
Hello Goodbye	Beatles
Higher And Higher	Jackie Wilson
How Can I Be Sure?	Rascals
I Am The Walrus	Beatles
I Say A Little Prayer	Dionne Warwick

I Second That Emotion	Smokie Robinson
I Was Made To Love Her	Stevie Wonder
I've Been Lonely Too Long	Rascals
Keep The Ball Rollin'	Jay/Techniques
Kentucky Woman	Neil Diamond
Kind Of A Drag	Buckinghams
Lazy Day	Spanky/Our Gang
Let's Spend The Night Together	Rolling Stones
Light My Fire	Doors
Love Is Here And Now You're Gone	Supremes
Love Is Strange	Peaches & Herb
Magical Mystery Tour	Beatles
Massachusetts	Bee Gees
Never My Love	Association
Penny Lane	Beatles
Please Love Me Forever	Bobby Vinton
Release Me	Englebert Humperdinck
Respect	Aretha Franklin
Ruby Tuesday	Rolling Stones
San Franciscan Nights	Animals
San Francisco	Scott McKenzie
She'd Rather Be With Me	The Turtles

War Years

Strawberry Fields Forever	Beatles
Sunday Will Never Be The Same	Spanky/Our Gang
Thank The Lord For The Nighttime	Neil Diamond
The Tracks of My Tears	Johnny Rivers
There's A Kind Of Hush	Herman's Hermits
To Sir With Love	Lulu
Tracks Of My Tears	Johnny Rivers
Up Up And Away	Fifth Dimension
White Rabbit	Jefferson Airplane
Windy	Association
Woman	Gary Puckett
Words Of Love	Mamas & Papas
Words	Monkees
You Got To Me	Neil Diamond
You Got What It Takes	Dave Clark Five
You Know What I Mean	Turtles
You're My Everything	Temptations
Your Precious Love	Marvin Gaye

News of interest to us in 1968...

●The first emergency 911 telephone system was installed in New York

●Green Bay beat Oakland in the second Super Bowl

●Oil was discovered in Alaska

●President Johnson decided not to run for another term as President

●North Korea captured the U.S.S. Pueblo and imprisoned the crew for eleven months

●Martin Luther King was assassinated in Memphis, Tennessee

●Senator Robert Kennedy was assassinated in California

●The Democratic convention in Chicago was disrupted by war protestors

●President Johnson halted the bombing in Vietnam to try to promote peace talks with the Vietnamese

●Richard Nixon defeated Vice-President Hubert Humphrey for President

●The Detroit Tigers won the World Series

●North Vietnam launched the TET offensive

●I began serving my tour of duty with the 25th Infantry Division in Vietnam

●The death toll in Vietnam approached 30,000 and we had 550,000 troops in the war

What I remember about 1968

Cost of Living in 1968	
Gallon of Milk	$1.21
Loaf of Bread	22¢
New Automobile	$2,450
Gallon of Gas	34¢
New Home	$40,000
Average Income	$6,244

In 1968, I was in Vietnam and music was not the most important thing on my mind. We got to hear the popular tunes periodically or read about them in the "Stars and Stripes". The "Stars and Stripes" newspaper was our only contact with the outside world except for the mail we received from home.

The top songs in 1968 were "Green Tambourine" by the Lemon Pipers, "Hello I Love You" by the Doors, "Hey Jude" and "Lady Madonna" by the Beatles.

Journey of a Baby Boomer

I was 22 years old, on my way to Vietnam when many of my friends were college seniors in 1968 and our favorite songs included:

Sittin' On The Dock Of The Bay	Otis Redding
A Beautiful Morning	Rascals
Ain't Nothing Like The Real Thing	Marvin Gaye
Always Something There To Remind Me	Dionne Warwick
Angel Of The Morning	Merrilee Rush
Autumn Of My Life	Bobby Goldsboro
Born To Be Wild	Steppenwolf
Bottle Of Wine	Jimmy Gilmer
Do You Know The Way To San Jose	Dionne Warwick
Dream A Little Dream Of Me	Mamas & Papas
For Once In My Life	Stevie Wonder
Goin' Out Of My Head Over You	Lettermen
Hello, I Love You	Doors
Hey Jude	Beatles
Hurdy Gurdy Man	Donovan
I Can't Stop Dancing	Archie Bell
I Gotta Get A Message To You	Bee Gees
I Heard It Through The Grapevine	Marvin Gaye

War Years

I Love How You Love Me	Bobby Vinton
I Wonder What She's Doing Tonight	Boyce & Hart
If I Were A Carpenter	Four Tops
Jumpin' Jack Flash	Rolling Stones
Lady Madonna	Beatles
Like To Get To Know You	Spanky
Love Child	Supremes
Midnight Confessions	Grassroots
Mrs. Robinson	Simon/Garfunkel
People Got To Be Free	Rascals
Put Your Head On My Shoulder	Lettermen
Scarborough Fair	Simon & Garfunkel
She's A Heartbreaker	Gene Pitney
The Dreams Of The Everyday Housewife	Glen Campbell
The Look Of Love	Sergio Mendes
The Unicorn	Irish Rovers
This Guy's In Love With You	Herb Alpert
Tighten Up	Archie Bell/The Drells
Turn Around, Look At Me	The Vogues
Valleri	Monkees
Walk Away Renee	Four Tops

Journey of a Baby Boomer

Wichita Lineman	**Glenn Campbell**
With A Little Help From My Friends	**Beatles**
Young Girl	**Gary Puckett**

News of interest to us in 1969...

●Sesame Street began on television

●Senator Ted Kennedy drove his car off a bridge on Chappaquiddick Island and Mary Jo Kopechne was killed

●I arrived home from Vietnam

●The U.S. wins the space race by landing a man on the moon

●Woodstock was held and over 500,000 attended

●Charles Manson and his cult murdered actress Sharon Tate and six others in what was called "Helter Skelter"

●Hurricane Camille hit the Mississippi gulf coast

●"The "Chicago 7" had their day in court

●The New York Mets won the World Series and the New York Jets won the Super Bowl led by quarterback Joe Namath

What I remember about 1969

Cost of Living in 1969	
Gallon of Milk	$1.26
Loaf of Bread	23¢
New Automobile	$2,475
Gallon of Gas	36¢
New Home	$40,000
Average Income	$6,460

I returned from Vietnam in 1969 to start life over with my wife and son. This meant returning to college, getting a job and supporting my family. Music wasn't as important to me as it once was. I had other things on my mind, but music seemed to help erase some of the unpleasant memories of the past year.

In 1969 the top songs were "A Time for Us" by Henry Mancini, "Aquarius" by the Fifth Dimensions, "Dizzy" by Tommy Roe, "Get Back" by the Beatles and "Honky Tonk Women" by the Rolling Stones.

War Years

**I was 23 years old, trying to put the war behind me
In 1969 and our favorite songs included:**

A Boy Named Sue	Johnny Cash
And When I Die	Blood, Sweat ,Tears
Aquarius/Let The Sunshine In	Fifth Dimension
Build Me Up Buttercup	Foundations
Come Together	Beatles
Crimson and Clover	Tommy James
Down On The Corner	Credence Clearwater
Easy To Be Hard	Three Dog Night
Everyday People	Sly/Family Stone
Get Back	Beatles
Gimmie Gimmie Good Lovin'	Crazy Elephant
Give Peace A Chance	John Lennon
Hooked On A Feeling	B.J. Thomas
Hot Fun In The Summertime	Sly/Family Stone
Hurt So Bad	Lettermen
I Started A Joke	Bee Gees
I'd Wait A Million Years	Grassroots
I'll Never Fall in Love Again	Tom Jones
I'm A Drifter	Bobby Goldsboro
In The Year 2525	Zager & Evans

In the Ghetto	**Elvis Presley**
Jean	**Oliver**
Lay Lady Lay	**Bob Dylan**
Leaving On A Jet Plane	**Peter, Paul & Mary**
Love Can Make You Happy	**Mercy**
Love Me Tonight	**Tom Jones**
Lucy In The Sky With Diamonds	**Beatles**
Midnight Cowboy	**Henry Mancini**
More Today Than Yesterday	**Spiral Staircase**
Proud Mary	**Credence Clearwater**
Put A Little Love In Your Heart	**Jackie DeShannon**
Smile A Little Smile For Me	**Flying Machine**
Someday We'll Be Together	**Supremes**
Spinning Wheel	**Blood, Sweat/Tears**
Stand By Your Man	**Tammy Wynette**
Sugar Sugar	**Archies**
Suspicious Minds	**Elvis Presley**
Sweet Caroline	**Neil Diamond**
Take A Letter Maria	**R.B. Greaves**
These Eyes	**Guess Who**
This Girl Is A Woman Now	**Gary Puckett**
This Magic Moment	**Jay/The Americans**

War Years

Time Of The Season	The Zombies
Tracy	Cuff Links
Try A Little Tenderness	Three Dog Night
What Does It Take	Jr. Walker/All Stars
When I'm Sixty-four	Beatles
Workin' On A Groovy Thing	Fifth Dimension
Worst That Could Happen	Brooklyn Bridge
Yester Me Yester You Yesterday	Stevie Wonder
You've Made Me So Very Happy	Blood/Sweat/Tears

My Story

Over the past three years I have attempted to put into words what my journey during the 1950's and 1960's was like. It has been fun, depressing at times and difficult for me to put in writing many of my memories. So much has happened over the last 50 years that volumes could and will be written by others. But, this has been *my story*.

My story revolves around my family. From my earliest memories Mom and Dad were there. They gave and gave to ensure we knew what family life was to be like. We ate, played and prayed together. They were patient, understanding and always supportive.

In 1962 I saw how unselfish they were when they adopted a little girl named Tanya. She became our sister and moved into a home full of love and encouragement. It wasn't until then that I actually realized what *unconditional love* meant. No greater love can be shown an individual than to give that person your life. Mom and Dad set the example for Buddy, Doug and me.

I have witnessed the influence of Mom and Dad on our lives in many ways. I remember Buddy giving his lunch to classmates in elementary school because they were too poor to bring a lunch. My brother Doug never forgets a family members' birthday or anniversary, comforts people who are grieving and is the most dependable person I have ever known.

Doug looked after Anne when I was in Vietnam. I will never forget his sacrifice for me. He meant so much to us during that time, that when our second son was born in 1970, we named him Doug in an effort to honor him.

Relationships like this don't just happen. They exist because of a commitment to the family. Commitment evolves because of deep caring for others and an outward expression of love to them. Mom and Dad taught us that.

As our children have gotten older and our family has grown, they now have the legacy of love and commitment to carry forward. Only unconditional love and commitment to one another can keep the true concept of family alive. It is my prayer that life for Jimmy and Joy, Doug and Holly, and Ben and Amanda will be filled with fun, happiness and love.

About the Author

James Fred Mitchell, Jr. *(Jim, also know as Butch by family and close friends)* is recognized across the country for his power packed presentations and storytelling. He has over twenty years experience as a professional speaker and speaks to thousands of individuals each year sharing with them the power he has found in humor.

His engagements range from entertaining and humorous keynote or banquet speeches to exciting seminar and adult education programs. He is the author of numerous professional development publications and three previous books **Snapshots of Chuckles & Laughs**, **Passport To Financial Freedom** and **Passport To Super Leadership**.

Jim is a decorated Vietnam War veteran having served with the 25th Infantry Division and the 82nd Airborne Division. He holds a Bachelor of Science degree in Accounting and both Master and Doctorate degrees in Theology. He is a member of the Rotary Club and the National Speakers Association. Jim and his wife, Anne live in Auburn, Alabama.

**For Information
About
Seminars and Keynote Speeches
Contact:**

**Jim Mitchell
Seminars & Presentation, LLC
2510 Wildwood Drive
Auburn, AL 36832
or
visit his web site:**

www.jimtalks.com

**Phone:(334) 887-6464
(800) 821-4851
fax(334) 826-8490
e-mail address: mitchelljf@usa.net**

Journey of a Baby Boomer

Other Publications By Jim Mitchell

<u>Snapshots of Chuckles & Laughs</u>

<u>Passport To Financial Freedom</u>

<u>Passport To Super Leadership</u>

Passport To Super Leadership
(Seminar Workbook)

Time Management For Entrepreneurs
(Seminar Workbook)

Passport To Customer Service Excellence
(Seminar Workbook)

Dealing With Difficult People
and Workplace Conflict
(Seminar Workbook)